Psychological Emergencies Of Childhood

GILBERT KLIMAN, M.D.

Director
The Center for Preventive Psychiatry
White Plains, New York

GRUNE & STRATTON, New York and London

First printing March 1968
Second printing February 1971

Grune & Stratton, Inc.
757 Third Avenue, New York, New York 10017

Library of Congress Catalog Card Number 67-22204
International Standard Book Number 0-8089-0234-2

Printed in the United States of America (C-C)

Contents

Dedication and Acknowledgments

MANY OF THE CASES described in this book are from the research and treatment files of The Center for Preventive Psychiatry, which was created to help well-functioning people who are experiencing situational crises. The research activities of The Center, especially its preschool program, are partly supported by The Foundation for Research in Preventive Psychiatry.

This book is dedicated to the staff of The Center for Preventive Psychiatry, without whom much of the work described would never have been done, and to the trustees of The Foundation for Research in Preventive Psychiatry—Marianne Kris, M.D., Mary O'Neil Hawkins, M.D., and Milton Berner—whose scientific, emotional and financial support made much of that work possible.

I am especially grateful to my wife, Ann Kliman, Research Associate of The Center, who did most of the interviews in our joint studies of healthy children's reactions to life crises (partly described in Chapter IV), and encouraged and helped me in the formation and workings of The Center. The contributions of Mrs. Doris Gorin to The Cornerstone School, a division of The Center, were intrinsic to the development of the technique described in Chapter II. To Myron Stein, M.D., who helped perform and shape The Center's psychoanalytic work from its inception, and to our teachers, therapists, and administrative staff, special thanks are also due.

Introduction

Psychological Emergencies of Childhood is intended as a guide for psychiatrists, pediatricians and educators oriented toward prevention of children's emotional disorders.

Sources from which case illustrations are drawn include patients from The Center for Preventive Psychiatry, from my own practice, and from a research project at The Albert Einstein College of Medicine, Department of Child Psychiatry, where the author and his wife investigated healthy children's reactions to the death of a parent.

This book emphasizes situations with clearly discernible external events such as death and severe illness in the family. There is special reason for such use of the external, though it goes hand in hand with careful attention to each child's and each family's unique means of coping with outer events. Beginning with externals, it is possible to lead the reader to more clearly understand internal aspects of psychological emergencies.

Sharply defined catastrophes provide tragic, but nevertheless important, natural laboratories for study and treatment of emotional disorder as it begins. In some cases a preventive opportunity is present which will never again be available. In other cases, preexisting problems are already severe but the new emergency presents opportunities for a child and his family to learn better ways of coping with their adaptive tasks. More often than regular office practice would reveal, a mildly neurotic child and family can rearrange their inner workings advantageously when fate provides an urgent challenge—a psychological emergency. Some general principles of preventive work will be dealt with in this regard.

No book on this subject can be complete if it fails to make clear the high prevalence of childhood psychological emergencies. The first chapter suggests a means for strengthening very young children's reactions to such inevitable emergencies before they occur. Granted that emergency events are common, preparedness is in order. For that reason, readers are urged to give this "immunizing" chapter their most sympathetic attention. This attention must be sympathetic, because the concepts and programs of prevention proposed there and in later parts of the book are opposed to many customary modes of psychological management when dealing with young children.

Later chapters contain clinical data, in which several cases of brief as well as prolonged intervention during pathogenic situations are sketched. To illustrate an especially avoided area of work with families in the midst of psychopathogenic experiences, some features of the analysis of a dying child are described.

It may be asked why much space has been given to the management of a dying child (Chapter II). There are two justifications. First, the situation is often an extreme psychological emergency. Second, the subject has been sharply avoided in most other works, and even when dealt with has usually been approached with deleterious hesitancy. For similar reasons, death of a parent has been given more emphasis than the much more common psychological emergency of divorce in the family. It is hoped that principles which emerge from these more stark areas will make up for the task's unpleasant aspects.

In most sections, before describing the author's own cases and methods, a review of relevant psychoanalytic literature is presented. The generally accepted term "trauma" will be used interchangeably with the phrase "pathogenic experience." The latter phrase is preferred because it is less concrete and implies personal psychological participation rather than the mechanical or anatomic connotations of trauma—"wound" or "damage." Trauma also has misleading connotations of overemphasizing the external process.

It is hoped that the reporting of emotional response to easily defined and verified realistic events will tend to be what Hartmann points out as an increasingly rare part of recent psychoanalytic work: observation where hypotheses are in the background rather than foreground (1958). If only one impression emerges from scrutiny of this book, hopefully it will be that the reader, like the author, finds himself in a region in which emotional forces have an awesome quality. Professional helpers who can achieve a perception of this quality of childhood psychological emergencies are better equipped to assist their child patients.

CHAPTER I

The Immunizing Value of Sharing Truths

THE CONCEPT of "psychological immunization" comes from a rather underdeveloped field in psychiatry—that part of preventive psychiatry which gives attention to the life-crises of well-functioning individuals. Attention to life crises has become imperative. Data has been collected concerning unusual psychological risks of children exposed to such experiences early in life as hospitalization, adoption, loss of a parent, or divorce in the family. In adulthood, also, the death of a spouse, divorce and serious illness of family members are hazards to emotional health. At The Center for Preventive Psychiatry we have extended our work to include individuals faced with many other psychological hazards: children confronted by the perplexities of a parent's mental illness, children facing their own fatal illness, and children who have witnessed crimes of violence or who themselves have been the victims of adult cruelty or rape.

Generally, one of the most significant accomplishments of preventive medicine has been the development of immunizing substances. Therefore it might be useful to state a general definition of immunization before proceeding with its psychiatric aspects. Immunization can be defined as a process which enables the host to cope with a noxious agent without becoming seriously ill. An immunizing substance may be the same as the agent which can produce an illness. A very small dose, for example, of attenuated viral or bacterial culture may produce a permanent or temporary immunity, whereas a very large dose given suddenly might produce an overwhelming illness. The concepts of dose and abruptness should be thought of in connection with the host-organism's resistance to the noxious agent. What is a fatal dose of bacterial culture or toxin for a child may be an immunizing or even therapeutic dose for an adult.

An early psychoanalytic concept with some relevance to immunization was developed by Freud in his *Project for a Scientific Psychology*. (1895). In this treatise Freud wrote of the desirability of exciting the perceptual, cognitive and adaptive apparatus of the mind into a state of readiness when faced by danger. Defensive excitation of the entire mental appartus into readiness is the prototype of psychological immunizing or preparing function. This simple idea of a state or readiness will be found of much value in daily work with young children. Later in this volume concrete examples will be given of how a state of readiness may be achieved in the face of external or internal danger, trauma, or even remote future trauma. Later Freud developed a concept called "signal anxiety"—such a low dose of anxiety that it is not consciously noted. It is thought of as a triggering or signaling process setting into motion useful defenses and adaptive mechanisms of the mind.

The concept of a low dose of anxiety is quite important in the effort to prepare children for the difficulties of life. It is to be contrasted with panic or catastrophic reactions, which involve high degrees of rapidly arising emotion and overwhelm the organism. Floods of anxiety may lead to a regression to primitive and pathologic mechanisms of adaptation.

The concept of "mastery in advance" is also valuable in developing a plan for psychological immunization. This concept includes active coping with stress before an event by reflection or fantasy and by actual experience with small doses of a stressful transaction. Planned preparation of preschool children for various life discomforts and dangers is advocated. The use of low doses of anxiety can be encouraged; through prior limited actual or mental experiences readiness for what life naturally has in store can be developed. The function of thought, with low doses of emotion, is emphatically important in this matter of mental preparedness or immunization. A useful theory of healthy adaptation must include the low quantity of energy involved in thought. Reflective thought (including fantasy) is a kind of "trial action." It proceeds with low quantities of psychological energy as compared to the energy required in action. It is one of man's most useful adaptive instruments.

No situations are better than those of mothers, preschool teachers, or pediatricians to provide a child with carefully supervised experience in "trial action" or thought preparatory to real life experience. In 1964 Mrs. Elissa Burian, Director of the Westchester Ethical Society Nursery School, White Plains, N.Y., Mrs. Doris Gorin and the author collaborated in a project designed to predict some aspects of the behavior of sixteen preschool children as they entered nursery school. At that time we tried in particular to predict responses to the situation of separation from mothers. As a side result of that project, we were impressed with how the life of an ordinary preschool child is filled with many large and small crises in a short period of time. We might have avoided recognizing, but were forced to notice, that the sixteen children in our study went through externally imposed torment within a two-week period. Every preschool teacher, should she look, would probably find that, within less than a semester, there are many serious illnesses, operations, deaths, moves, losses of pets, and other strains within the families of her pupils.

The most serious of the childhood crises mentioned is the death of a parent. By kindergarten age almost one child in twenty in our nation has lost one or both parents by death. The percentage is lower among upper-class families, where the death of parents tends to occur rarely during early childhood. But among lower-class families parental death is quite frequent by kindergarten age (exceeding five per cent). Separation, divorce and adoption are even more common. Less likely to be pathogenic, but still painful and frequent, are transient parents, death of grandparents, birth of siblings, and (often not thought of) deformities and physical and mental handicaps of family members.

Educators will be particularly interested to know that learning difficulties often seem connected with the failure of families to help the child to slowly learn about such certain disturbing realities of the family environment. An example is a seven-year-old patient with severe inability to read and associated anxiety about "looking." It became clear during the course of his analysis that a codeterminant (certainly not the sole determinant) of his learning inhibition was that his father was blind in one eye. The child, although perceiving there was something wrong with his father's vision, could not speak of it to the father. His father would not initiate the conversation, and the boy soon learned that he dare not discomfort him by asking. This situation interfered with solution of the child's oedipal problems, and even had special connections to the legend of Oedipus.

Among other experiences known which concern learning difficulties is that of a dreadful circumstance in the life of a seven-year-old girl who required treatment for a severe learning inhibition. When she was two years old, the child either pushed or was present when another two-year-old child fell over the edge of a cliff. The other child was killed. The family moved away from the neighborhood and did not discuss the reasons for this move. At that time the girl was barely speaking in small paragraphs. It was rationalized by her parents that because she could not fully comprehend this event they would not even partly explain its nature. However, some five years later it was quite helpful to her (even though she could not even remember a single detail) to have family conferences in which the entire episode was talked over in a factual manner, a little bit at a time. It would have been helpful for that child had she been gradually introduced to the realities of the situation much earlier.

Similar situations arise frequently in families with alcoholic parents. The parents' incomprehensible behavior is never discussed. The erratic hours, temperament and attentiveness of such parents are hardly ever explained to the children. Yet the children are constantly perplexed by the variegated environment to which they must adapt. Often communication does take place. Surely the preschool child whose parent is alcoholically agitated is receiving a communication, but it is not verbal communication. It is communication through perception of behavior. It occurs without benefit of a structure of preexisting worldliness and intellectual information with which the child can think rationally instead of simply perceive and puzzle unaided.

Perception of perplexing adult action is extravagant in the psychological economy of the child when it takes place in a setting of unreadiness. It would be economical even for a preschool child to talk and hear about alcoholism or drug-addiction rather than puzzle his way through raw perceptions, unaided by relevant knowledge. Verbal communication from a friendly, affectionate adult would provide emotional support and at the same time reduce the energy needed to cope with the experience.

Bereavement and Breakdown of Communication

Relevant material on communication problems has come from the results of a project which studied presumably well-functioning families whose sole reason for being studied was that a parent recently died. This study is described in detail in Chapter III. The families were presumably not unusual. Since there is reason to believe that an undue proportion of the children studied were already emotionally disturbed, we must consider the possibility that the post-bereavement breakdowns in emotional communication (which will be described) were a codetermining factor in the emotional problems.

Three families with preschool children will be sketched here to illustrate communication problems.

A case of severe communication problem is that of a father who called from and was conferred with at a funeral parlor 24 hours after his wife and son died in a car crash. On a conscious level his emergency was that he had not been able to tell his two daughters, who were in the same crash, that their mother and brother had died. They had witnessed the bodies being taken away in an ambulance. Nothing had really escaped their perceptions. But the father had told them that the brother and mother were in a hospital and that they might get better. Fortunately he tried to approximate some of the serious aspects of the tragic event. The consequences of even such temporary withholding of information may include some splitting of the sense of reality from the sense of what is permissible to know, think, feel and communicate socially. Later the schism between memory and communication became more severe because the father could not tolerate the girls' mentioning the mother to him for some years thereafter. The entire past of the little girls was clouded over not only with sadness but also with the communication problem which made them partially devalue and isolate their own histories.

In another family a three-year-old girl witnessed the accidental drowning of her father. She was present during the resuscitation effort. However, as soon as it was found that the father could not be revived, the child was whisked away and kept out of the house for five days. She had no physical contact or other communication with the mother. The close friend with whom the child stayed told her nothing except that the mother was very busy. It was five days before the mother could bring herself to either see the child or tell that her father had died.

In another case a father had what was thought to be a mild virus. His temperature rose and he was hospitalized. The child, who was four years old, was told that daddy had been taken to the hospital. There was no serious anxiety since the illness was thought to be very mild. The father died very unexpectedly. The child was taken out of the house to an aunt's residence, was kept there for three days and was given no further information. When he asked how daddy was, he was told that daddy was in the hospital and that the doctors were working with him. Not until two days after the funeral was he told that his father had died.

In another family with preschool children, communication was indirect. The mother discovered that she had a very serious illness which required hospitalization, surgery, and postsurgical treatment. During a period of several weeks prior to hospitalization she talked freely on the telephone, with the children clustered around her or in the next room, giving full details of exactly what had happened and what would happen. But there never was any direct communication with the children to tell them that she would have to go to the hospital and would be there for several weeks. The mother seemed unaware that the children had picked up a tremendous amount of information from telephone conversations. The children became upset but were unable to verbalize their feelings because the adult had not made it possible or permissible to do so.

In each of the above families, adults seemed unaware that a child was picking up nonverbal information. In each case a child was suddenly aware that he was taken out of the home. The situation changed radically. Suddenly there were people rushing into the house, additional phone calls, and much adult activity and agitation, but communication with the children was faulty.

Psychological Immunization in the Classroom

A useful focus for preventive work with very young children is in the nursery or kindergarten classroom. The Cornerstone School at The Center for Preventive Psychiatry provides classroom settings for a program of preventive and psychoanalytic treatment of preschool children. In addition to treatment of underlying problems in that setting, innumerable opportunities arise to communicate forthrightly.

Experiences occur in classroom life about which adults might ordinarily tend to avoid talking. For instance, if a child is absent on a particular day, the staff makes sure that sometime during the course of that day the absence of the child is discussed. First, an opportunity is given to mention spontaneously the missing child. If there is no spontaneous mention, the topic is then mentioned by the teacher or analyst. Ususally, children like to call an absent child on the telephone to find out what is wrong and to talk with him. Even more meaningful is a teacher's absence, and it is especially important to discuss the children's fantasies and real reasons why the teacher is not present. A teacher is so important to each child that it would be peculiar not to acknowledge the fact of her absence.

Minor instances in which communication might ordinarily be avoided by adults are worthy of attention in such a setting, and probably in any setting where a child is dealing with pressing emotional matters. The use of an open sharing approach in seemingly minor matters will build greater sharing ability in the child. For example, a child was restless but uncommunicative in a situation where his mother had dropped him off at school. Her car remained in the school's parking lot. The lot was visible from the classroom window. Although the child did not comment, his restlessness was apparent. When it was discussed with the child that his mother's car was still in view, it turned out he certainly did know she was there and had seen the car a number of times during his restless period. He was not ready to talk about the matter spontaneously, yet was relieved to have it brought up.

A teacher or pediatrician can provide a real-life model for coping with painful realities forthrightly. The pediatrician or teacher may also provide a vote of confidence in a child's ability to face and deal with a painful reality. Naturally opportunities to share and ventilate a child's distress are also provided. This is a proper role for the pediatrician or teacher—to receive outbursts of emotion, preferably verbally expressed. But one should not be too ambitious in this regard. The goal is to create a climate in which communication can occur without forcing a child.

Sometimes a psychological emergency occurs right in the classroom. In one instance an assistant teacher fell and fractured her ankle in the classroom. The children had been playing with water. The tile floors became slippery, especially where soap had been spilled. In an effort to dry the soapy area and make it safe, the teacher herself slipped. (There was no doctor in the class at that moment.) The head teacher perceived that the assistant was in pain: "I had no idea of the extent of her injury, but what I decided to do was to get the children to be with us there while I asked her how she was feeling. They sat, they helped, they asked her how she was. They expressed the concern they had. One of them brought a chair for her. They sat by. Some were quiet. Some were able to talk with her, and we included the entire group in the situation. She told them how she was feeling, that it did hurt and that she wasn't sure she could move."

One child in particular seemed to profit especially from this shared classroom emergency. This was a child who needed help in dealing with what for his parents was the particularly painful fact of his having been adopted. Some discussion on this subject had already been established. It was only a short time later that the child's adoptive father was admitted to a hospital for orthopedic work. It appeared to us that the child's verbalization about his father's operation was unusually complete for this often nonverbal boy. Still later, the child observed a man who some months before had a leg amputated. Despite a high baseline level of castration anxiety in his mental life, the child was able to walk up to the man, ask about the leg, and get a very sensible and reasonable communication from the amputee. Apparently the child elicited an understanding from the man that he was a child who was ready to talk about facts. Another child would probably have elicited a slightly different response. Perhaps the amputee recognized from his experience with other children that the child's questioning was anxiety-tolerant. After the child's experience with the amputee, he came back to the assistant teacher (who by now had returned to the classroom) and checked with her his fantasy that she might now have an artificial leg. It seemed that this fantasy—of the teacher's healing leg being artificial—was one which other children might also develop but which would have remained underground and have pathologic implications to a greater degree than under these circumstances of sharing with helpful adults.

Among the major tragic events which have happened to families in The Cornerstone School was one which was especially unexpected: the death of a child's father six weeks after the beginning of school. The death occurred in a car accident over which the man had no control. Since the community at large was increasingly in possession of this information and it was not privileged, the matter was brought to the attention of each family member of the school. Each mother decided to tell her own child of the death, so that when the children arrived in school the next day they were all informed. The child whose father had died also came to school. There was a good deal of talk about the death between him and the other children with direct questioning as well as play-communication. It seemed that the experience of other children being frank in their questions about the topic was of some help to the bereaved child. Since there is weakness in children's ability to deal with adults in direct talk, the bereaved child's transactions with the other children were somewhat comparable to speaking of the problem in the third person as a technique in treatment. It kept the dose low, diluting the noxious affects and thoughts. Another diluting factor was that there were other children present who could recognize and state that their fathers also had died. It relieved the bereaved child of the necessity for saying everything himself. He could pick up from where other children had left off. Also, his perception that other children were allowed to communicate about this issue may have removed some of his undesirable feelings of specialness and isolation.

Prior to the above-mentioned parental death, there had been several incidents of deaths of pets in the school's families. In each instance the families had difficulty dealing with the pet's death. One father secretly flushed a turtle down the toilet, and remarked to the child's teacher that his boy "never talked about it—probably didn't even care." The matter of the turtle's death and disposal without communication was interpreted to his family as an instance in which the child's silence was mistakenly equated with lack of thought and feeling.

Another parent who also had a turtle die brought a question to the teacher as to whether the turtle should just be thrown away or buried with the child's knowledge. These seemingly mundane domestic experiences proved to have some immunizing value, especially since the father of one of the "turtle boys" was the one who died. We had, in fact, already helped the not-yet-deceased father acknowledge the death of the turtle. It may have been useful to this bereaved family that they had been immunized a little bit in facing death. The mother spontaneously acknowledged to the teacher that it had been good that she had been helped to deal with the turtle. Naturally, evaluating the importance of such minor immunizations must be rather guarded. For example, in the bereaved family, it had taken weeks for the parents to acknowledge that the turtle had died. Their focus of defensive noncommunication then became the fact that it had been flushed down the toilet, a fact which remained a permanently unshared unpleasantness. Similarly, the father's mode of burial remained unshared in this family, although there was some reason to believe that the child had knowledge of it.

No matter what the conscious or unconscious attitudes of adults are in the immunizing process, they are frequently misunderstood by children. The child may misperceive or misunderstand in a way over which the parent, pediatrician or teacher has little control. Certainly adults should not hold themselves responsible for failing to overcome such difficulties. Anna Freud tells of a tragic murder in which a little girl's mother was killed by her father. The mother, who had been stabbed, did not die immediately. She ran to the little girl, who was then three years old. In her effort to protect the child against death from the berserk father, the mother said "Get out! Get out!" All the child seemed to understand of the event was that the mother had told her to "go away" and then had gone away herself. It took a great deal of work to overcome the child's distortions of that reality, although, of course, many other surrounding and pre-existing difficulties disposed the child to unreadiness to assimilate the gruesome and savage deprivation she had experienced (Freud, A., in Bergen, 1958).

Not long after the death of a father, tragedy struck our school once more. The educational director's husband died, also quite unexpectedly. This was an event which affected all of our staff profoundly, and did not escape the children—for the educational Director was also a teacher. The author learned the news while in the classroom, having received a telephone call and then having the awesome task of communicating the news to his friend and colleague.

There was little deviation from our theme of communication in this experience. After private communication, the analyst and teacher approached the children. It was explained that the teacher had received some bad news and had to leave school early. She was very upset, they were told, and would be able to tell them more about it in a short while. Each child responded in his individual fashion, but in a way which led us to believe that they felt encouraged to know that the adults trusted them by giving them some explanation. The next day, when the teacher was able to speak to the children, she told them of her husband's death, a fact which they had already learned from their own families. There were many discussions and myriad reverberations in the psychological life of each child—much of it analyzable. The frankness of the children's responses seemed useful as well as heartening. Growth and apparently little regression followed this sad episode. It would be hard to understand how the children could not have regressed under the impact of this event, so shortly following the ankle accident and the death of one child's father, had they not already been immunized by doses of truthful communications. There was all-too-painful firsthand evidence that the immunization procedure was working and useful at the preschool level, even with severe experiences of personal tragedy.

A major psychological immunization opportunity on a national level was forced upon us when teachers and parents were called upon to discuss with their children the assassination of President John F. Kennedy and the events which surrounded that assassination (see Chapter VIII). Preschool children, as well as much older ones, were hearing all about a murder and a funeral. There was widespread communication about such facts as the existence of a "catafalque" and the lowering of a coffin into a grave. Dealing with the death of a national figure, an important but distant person, had an immunizing value because of the low-dose level. Distance became a shielding or attenuating factor. Similarly, the death of a distant relative, or even a loved grandparent is usually an emotional experience of a weaker strength than that of a parent's death. Straightforward participation and some age-appropriate knowledge of the realities in these events is helpful for preschool children. (Further work along such lines will be described in Chapter III.)

A fact to be considered in the immunizing process is that what is experienced on a low-dose level is not simply an external event, but more an internal response to that event. Much of the internal response may be a reaction of protest and anger. There may be protest against the pain of the reality, and anger against the objects who are lost or who otherwise disappoint the child. What often compounds a child's anger is not only being left by the person who died or is ill, but also not being allowed full participation in the remaining parts of family life. Sometimes a child is shuffled off to unimportant neighborhood figures or to casual friends when there is a funeral or a visit to a sick relative. The child then experiences isolation from the most important people in his life. He may have no outlet for his own emotions even though other members of his family are free to share their turmoil with each other. Perhaps the adults may even keep themselves from expressing emotion in front of the child, so that he is further bewildered—as if no one really cares about what is happening.

To close this section with consideration of events which will provide frequent bases for psychological immunizing procedures, brief reference will be made to situations in the lives of an unselected group of regular nursery-school children studied by the author for a two-week period with the help of Mrs. Elissa Burian and Mrs. Doris Gorin.

There were only sixteen children in this group, but within a two-week period the following events were recorded in the children's lives: a tonsillectomy, the injury of a relative in a car crash, sudden hospitalization of a sister in the middle of the night, a brother's operation, the death of a grandmother, a prolonged parental absence due to a two-month trip abroad, the death of a turtle, the death of a cat, and revelation to a child's family that an uncle had died during the preceding month. Several weeks later an aunt died and a child's cousin had a hernia operation (both in the same family). Considering that only sixteen children were involved in this informal study, and that some events probably escaped the researcher's notice, there appears a rather high incidence level of life's crises. Yet, it is probably not an unusual series. It is, after all, impressive to think of the number of aunts, uncles, cousins, grandparents, neighbors, friends, siblings, and classmates in one child's life.

The opportunities provided for psychological strengthening through the process of immunization are apparently myriad. One may question whether they should be utilized, but there can be no question that the opportunities exist. It is hoped that others will give favorable consideration to the process as being desirable for even the youngest children, and that in time there will be an organized collection of data about differing techniques and results.

CHAPTER II

Illness in the Family

When a Child is Ill

CONSIDERABLE psychoanalytic and pediatric literature exists on this subject. A sampling given now will be a useful introduction to the case material and principles of advising parents which follow later in this chapter.

Childhood Bodily Illness, Hospitalization and Surgery.

Anna Freud (1952) goes beyond the usual discussion of the separation experience which occurs when hospitalization takes place. She discusses the effects of nursing, medical and surgical procedures.

First, there is a change of parental emotional climate during illness so that the child experiences unexpected handling such as deception, forced feeding, or forced bowel evacuation. He may react to such unexpected handling by feeling helpless and bewildered because he notices that formerly "immovable emotional and moral standards" are broken. Another extreme procedure may be the unexpected indulgence of the child's wishes, which makes it difficult for him to give up the incidental emotional gains after recovery. The experience of being nursed may be harmful to children who, because of their early stage in life, have recently been mastering various bodily functions. Nursing in which the child is fed, cleaned and assisted with excretory activities, his nakedness on view, is experienced as a loss of control in a variety of areas in which he has only recently learned control, with resultant pull toward earlier and more passive levels of development.

Two extremes of pathology may result. Children whose defenses against passive leaning and regressive pulls are very strong tend to become very obstinate, intractable patients. Others may lapse into a state of helpless infancy from which they reluctantly or never fully emerge.

Another category of pathogenic experience is restriction of movement and diet, which frequently occurs during illness. A number of authors have observed the consequences of extreme restraint in physical activity. Tic-like movements elsewhere in the body have been noted upon extreme restraint of limbs (Levy, 1945). In contrast to this involuntary and rather automatic limited muscular response, there may be more global involvement of the child as in rages and temper tantrums. The latter appear especially when mechanical deprivations beyond the customary expected medical procedures are unexpectedly heaped upon the child. Bergmann[5] notes that the restraint placed on one limb may lead to inhibition of movement in other unaffected parts. Yet certain ego-skills such as speech may undergo a rapid development, apparently in compensation for motor restriction of even one limb.

Anna Freud also discusses the effect of surgical operations. Such procedures often precipitate ideas and feelings of being attacked, overwhelmed or castrated. The actuality of surgery lends "a feeling of reality to the repressed fantasies, thereby multiplying the anxieties connected with them." When a child's defenses, for whatever reason, are unable to deal with the massive anxiety released, the operation is psychologically damaging.

In 1958 the American Psychoanalytic Association held a panel discussion, "Psychological Consequences of Physical Disease in Childhood" (Calef, 1959). The participants focused on instinctual vicissitudes under circumstances of varying bodily insults. A panel member, Dr. Anita Bell, described a compulsive, emotionally withholding and masochistic "bobbysoxer" with intractable asthma dating back to age two. The child was subjected to several major deprivation and interference experiences. At the age of five months, the patient's mother began holding a small receptacle to the anus whenever signs of defecating appeared. At ten months, upon development of eczema, the child's hands were bound, food was restricted, and she was kept in bed. Dr. Bell postulated that the girl was deprived of adequate anal-zone discharge opportunities. Oral-zone "premastery" was interfered with by the motor and food restrictions which followed the onset of eczema. Regression to the earliest respiratory phase then occurred—the phase in which "the child could be in control by holding her breath." Interference with the development of premastery activities in the anal and oral spheres was thought to have prevented fusion of libidinal and aggressive energies, and consequently interference with object-relations and the development of a masochistic pattern occurred.

Much of the material presented by other panel participants elaborated and extended Anna Freud's schematic work (Freud, A., 1952), to which L. Jessner added especially rich documentation and confirmation. Jessner concluded that since a child's parents are devalued through their helplessness to prevent the child's suffering and also are separated from the child, a kind of grief reaction occurs on both counts. The outcome, through reincorporation of the loved object, may spur maturation and improve realistic relation to the self and the parents.

Another panel member, Emmy Sylvester, emphasized the effects of mechanical contraptions which diminish pleasure and increase tension in a given body area. Unless alternate channels of discharge develop, redistribution of cathexes may occur regressively to "resomatization of the sense of self, reversal of outgoing libidinal strivings, and primitivization of ego functions and modes of object relation." The degree of psychological damage depends on (1) whether there is specific interference with the libidinal needs which happens to be ascendant, (2) the magnitude of mechanical restrictions, and (3) the capactiy for adaptation. The latter parallels the stage of object-relationship formation, strength of tension tolerance, and flexibility of energy discharge modes. Developmental interference experiences due to mechanical gadgets may be specific to the gadget's location. An infant whose severely infected mouth was stuffed with medicated cotton was fed by dropper; he later avoided exploration of the world by putting things in his mouth. Other reactions are unrelated to the gadget's location, depending on the phase of development. For example, a two-year-old boy with hip deformity mastered braces in a few hours, but lost his recent phase-specific achievement of bowel control. (Apparently although the panel did not discuss this point, it is clear that in the first case, where the reaction was considered specific to the gadget's location in the child's mouth, it might also be considered to be specific to the then-ascendant phase —the oral-exploratory.)

The panel advised that further study of psychological consequences of childhood illnesses should proceed more vigorously. Considerable opportunities exist for illuminating effects on differentiation of ego-functions. It was suspected that the paucity of recorded observation in the area may reflect cultural attitudes toward handicapped and physically damaged children, including deep-seated horror and resentment shared by analysts as well as parents. Dr. Marianne Kris[36] has observed that weakness in another human being excites in the perceiver a conflict about his own aggressive impulses. Perhaps such responses may lead to inhibition of constructive professional activity.

Congenital deformity—a case of phocomelia. Naturally, more is involved in congenital deformity or later childhood mutilation, than just the experience of interference with the body image. Anna Freud, in commenting on the case of a congenitally deformed boy, states that disabled people tend to "masochistic satisfaction, passivity, or self pity . . ." (Lussier, 1960). However, a contrary case is reported by Lussier of a boy whom Miss Freud examined and found to be actively oriented and not seeking pity.

Peter, age thirteen when beginning analysis, had been born with "malformed shoulders and abnormally short arms terminating in hands having only three fingers and no thumbs." At thirteen years, this shoulder-to-fingertip length measured only eight inches. Presenting problems included enuresis dating back to surgical preparation for artificial arms at age nine, backwardness at school, depressive tendencies, and an intense involvement in fantasies. Analysis revealed a powerful denial of handicap, with fantasies of superior physical abilities, such as becoming a champion tree-climber, tree-cutter, bicyclist and trumpeter. He had a strong desire for his mother to be "thrilled" by his frenzied physical (fantasy) performances, which usually ended up with a fantasy of a broken leg. The sexualization of physical-activity fantasies was so intense that he would "feel too hot and excited" to sleep if he thought them in bed.

A special feature of this boy's psychology was the amount of constructive use he made of his fantasies. Instead of serving only as substitutes for real gratifications, they became springboards for them. He actually learned to play a trumpet, joined a band, rode a bicycle, became a fisherman, swam and became a certified life-saver—he transformed pre-existing "fantasies into ego abilities."

One result of Peter's congenital handicap was "an unconscious feeling of incompleteness" and feminity "expressing itself endlessly in attempts to compensate for his deformity." Lussier predicts that this tendency will continue with repetition of achievements needed throughout the boy's life. Peter also possessed a special intolerance of his passive wishes, which led to termination of his analysis—to assuming independence of his analyst.

Childhood leg amputation. Emma Planck (1961) gives an account (in some detail) of a four-year, two-month-old patient, Ruthie, who was observed before and after having her leg amputated. Preventive psychotherapy was administered in a hospital play group several times a week for five weeks to prepare her for the loss of her limb. By that time she was suffering from gangrene below the knee and had no sensation in that area. Ruthie strenuously changed the subject when this fact was mentioned verbally. However, she spontaneously spoke of a doll who was going to have an operation; this lead was followed by the therapist who then constructed a special prosthesis doll which would undergo amputation and receive an artificial limb. With this doll, Ruthie revealed denial that she wished to walk again, plus a hope that another leg could be grown. Actively mastering the surgery in advance, Ruthie spent hours examining the doll, removing and replacing its artificial leg.

Following surgery, Ruthie occasionally wet and soiled herself. On occasion she refused food. Masturbation became more overt [a phenomenon also reported by Robertson (1956) in an account of her daughter's tonsillectomy]. Ruthie, like the Robertson child, wished to actively throw away the diseased part of the body. Five months passed before a prosthesis could be fitted, but it was accepted avidly and used with agility. Planck gives the impression that the regressive phenomena cleared, and "a warm, likable little girl emerged who could form positive trusting relationships to the unavoidably large number of people who had to care for her."

CASE REPORTS AND REVIEW OF THE LITERATURE ON TONSILLECTOMY: A Common Opportunity for Preventive Work

Reviewing emotional reactions of children to tonsillectomy and adenoidectomy, Anna Freud (1952) notes that the "traumatic potentialities" of such procedures lie principally in three factors: the anesthesia experience, the hospitalization experience, and the operative procedure itself. She finds that it is not "the castration fear, but the feminine castration wish in a male child" which most often leads to harmful psychological effects of a surgical procedure. The child either submits to the surgery as if it were seduction to passivity or else has to build up "permanent pathologically strong defenses" against his passive wish. Miss Freud here does not comment upon the traumatic effects of surgery in little girls. Regarding the effects of pain on children, Miss Freud notes that children she has observed who are "tough" in the face of pain are so because their "latent unconscious fantasies are less dominant and they are less apt to be connected with pain."

Jessner, Blom and Waldfogel (1952) demonstrate again that the prior state of the child is a major determinant of his response to this particular burden. Observations on 143 children, aged three to fourteen, revealed that tonsillectomy was stressful for each child. It generally activated fantasies of abandonment, mutilation and death, as well as bodily transformations and pregnancy. Most children integrated the experience successfully so far as immediate reaction was concerned. Prior experience with surgery sometimes heightened anxiety but improved the children's ability to "cope with the later operation." The authors suspect that these children knew that the "reality of such an event was not as terrible as their anticipating fantasies."

In contrast to the findings of Levy (1945), who studied younger children, age and sex did not appear to be significant factors in the severity of reactions to tonsillectomy. However, there was a marked shift in the focus of anxiety with age. Below age five, the event of hospitalization, together with its implication of separation from the family, was the main source of dread. However, by age ten to thirteen, the anesthesia experience was the focus of anxiety. Where the operations became a disturbing or disruptive experience, there was generally a pre-existing neurotic trend. Where there was not a prior neurotic trend, the newly disturbed children tended to have experienced "but not integrated" some threatening life situation such as the death of a relative. The authors believe that for children with pre-existing neurotic trends or disastrous life experiences not yet integrated, "preparation of the conventional kind did little to increase their capactiy to withstand" the surgery. For such children preventive intervention is advised in the form of "working through some of their deeper anxieties. Where there is evidence of a personality disturbance or a history of recent traumatic events in a child's life, careful consideration should be given to his emotional status with the view of postponing the operation or of taking psychotherapeutic measures." Failure of a child to indicate anxiety is also a bad prognostic sign. Overcontrol of fear, suppression, denial and avoidance of anxiety-related topics are measures which are liable to "collapse with a bang."

Regarding the prevention of pathologic consequences, Jessner concludes that the presence of a child's mother overnight in the hospital was not necessarily helpful to him although the mother's presence was certainly comforting against "fear of abandonment." A nurse might very well substitute for the mother. The child should feel that one nurse in particular is his protector although he could share with other childen.

Other measures advocated to prevent psychological damage from a tonsillectomy include the acknowledgment ". . . . of fear and expression of anxiety in play and talk. . . . Encouraging the child to express his feeling should, however, not be understood as inviting the child to give up control completely." An exceptionally helpful mechanism is the reversal of passive roles into active ones. Children should be helped to play the "surgeon or protecting mother with a doll or another young child.

Psychological preparation of a child for tonsillectomy: One especially illuminating example occurred in a family advised by a psychiatrist that preventive work prior to surgery might be useful for their eight-year-old boy. It was first ascertained that the family pediatrician and surgeon all were unwaveringly convinced of the necessity for the tonsillectomy and adenoidectomy to cure the child's adenoidal speech, snoring and frequent sore throats. (This procedure is performed on children with excessive frequency.) History from the parents revealed that the boy had been functioning fairly well socially and academically, although he was immature in several ways—especially in brevity of attention-span and inability to sit still. He occasionally appeared very stupid to his family and teachers, although he obtained good grades and had a high I.Q. His parents felt that his attitude toward the impending operation was generally favorable. He expected improvement in speech, and that his snoring would stop. He knew his older brother and sister had had tonsillectomies and both had become healthier and sturdier after surgery. Previous separation and physical pain experiences were limited. (At age five, he had run over a bunch of apples on his bicycle and had been badly bruised in the fall. At age eight, he had kicked a beehive accidentally and received one hundred stings! That same year a small piece of a fingertip was severed in a fall.)

Two interviews were held with the boy prior to surgery. He was alert, friendly, and clearly oriented to the purpose of our work. Preoperative procedures included the following:

1. Discussion with the boy of his own personality and interests as he viewed them, and of his general life situation.
2. Elicitation of his ideas of the anatomy of the tonsils and adenoids and of reasons for the proposed surgery.
3. Brief "correction" of misconceptions expressed.
4. Elicitation of his ideas of the technique of anesthesia and surgery.
5. Encouragement of the child's taking roles of the anesthetist and surgeon in fantasy and artistic description.

The child informed me that his "tonsils were too big and would have to come out," but was not sure how they caused problems. He also revealed that he had "three" tonsils, and made a drawing (upon request) to illustrate (see Fig. 1). The resemblance of his "tonsils" to male genitals was marked. (This resemblance is even more clear in Fig. 2.) I pointed out the resemblance to him, and later got his permission to share this confusion with his parents in case they could help him understand. I told him sometimes boys were worried that harm would come to other parts of their body during surgery, even to their penis and testicles, but that this would not happen He then informed me that the operation would be done with a dentist's drill, after he was "put to sleep." Brief efforts were made to correct his anatomical, surgical and anesthetic misconceptions. (See Fig. 3 for the patient's sketch of how he imagined the operation would be done.)

A postoperative followup was scheduled so that we could talk more about these matters. At that time the mother reported he had calmly told her he was "worried because Dr. Kliman had told him his balls (pointing between his legs) would be cut off." His mother—who had been with us when we discussed the similarity of his tonsils' drawing to a drawing of a penis and testicles— helped him correct this idea. The child came in to tell me that he felt fine, and that when meeting me before he had been "very upset and thought the doctor might take out

FIG. 1—"TONSILS." PREOPERATIVE SKETCH BY 8-YEAR-OLD BOY.

FIG. 2—PREOPERATIVE SKETCH. PROFILE BY THERAPIST; TONSILS BY PATIENT.

too much." He also reviewed some preoperative bad dreams which had occurred before his first visit with me. The dreams were of "bad animals coming in to the house." Disappointed to some extent, he believed he still snored despite the surgery. A postoperative misconception was that his "soft palate" might have been removed during the operation "because it would block air if it hangs down." The castration anxiety implied in such misconceptions makes followup meetings desirable from a preventive viewpoint. His idea that his postoperative drawing (Fig. 4) looked more like a girl than a boy is a further indication of the desirability of followup with this child whose misunderstandings and anxieties might ordinarily have passed unnoticed.

Psychological help with postoperative complications: As described in the case of an eight-year-old who underwent tonsillectomy, the tendency of young children to "genitalize" the area undergoing surgery is quite marked. A three-year-old boy who had an appendectomy displayed this "genitalizing" phenomenon quite strongly, but in regard to the intravenous feeding he received rather than to the surgical site itself.

Everett's appendectomy was followed by peritoneal infection and abscess formation. He received numerous intravenous injections and ate very

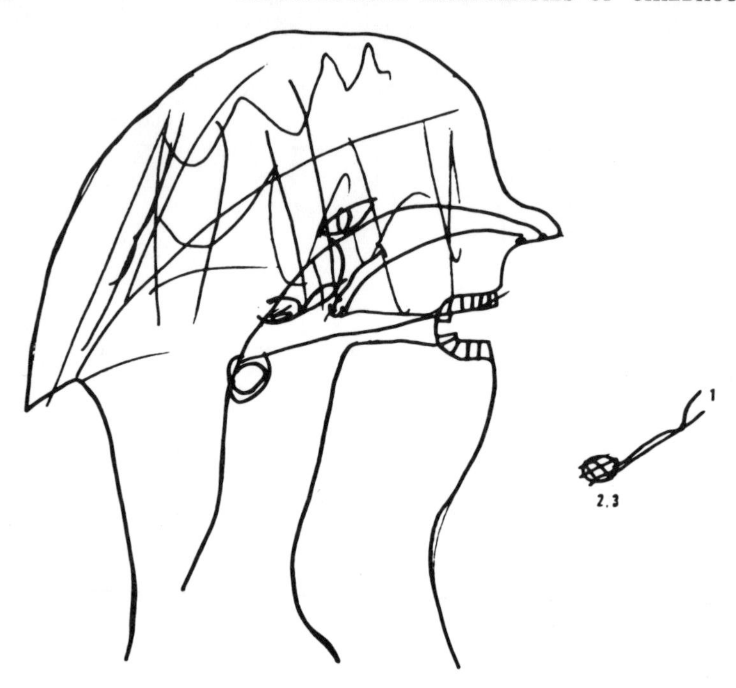

FIG. 3—"HOW THE OPERATION IS DONE." PREOPERATIVE SKETCH BY 8-YEAR-OLD BOY. 1: SPECIAL HANDLE TO MAKE LOOP CLOSE HARD AND FAST ON TONSILS. 2: LOOP TO REMOVE TONSILS. 3: "FAST OR SLOW MAKES NOT FEELING IT."

little for about five days postoperatively. Hospitalization was almost two weeks in duration, following which he was somewhat more withdrawn and quiet than previously. He also had a fear of sleeping without a night light (never a problem previously) and expressed anxiety about a playmate's fire truck—especially the thin hose with which it was equipped. Everett's mother had suspected, before the author was consulted, that this specific anxiety about the hose was because of associations with the intravenous tubing to which Everett had been attached for several days. The hose and the intravenous tubing were of about the same thickness.

In brief psychotherapy, Everett was able to communicate that he had worries about many playroom objects possibly being broken. In a spontaneous drawing of a duck, he emphasized that he knew ducks have tails, thus suggesting to the therapist that concerns over body integrity and specifically breaks and absences in the lower body regions must be dominating his mental life.

In response to the therapist's efforts to talk about and draw his recent hospital experiences, Everett became quite interested in directing the therapist just how to draw the room in which he had been confined for two weeks (see Fig. 5). The boy should be in bed, with a table next to the bed, and a nurse should be standing there—smiling. The nurse is nice, but she comes to give the boy a shot in the belly, and then in the space between his belly and his arm—into the bed. Then the patient indicated by touching the drawing, that the nurse gives the boy a "shot" in his crotch (see Fig. 6).

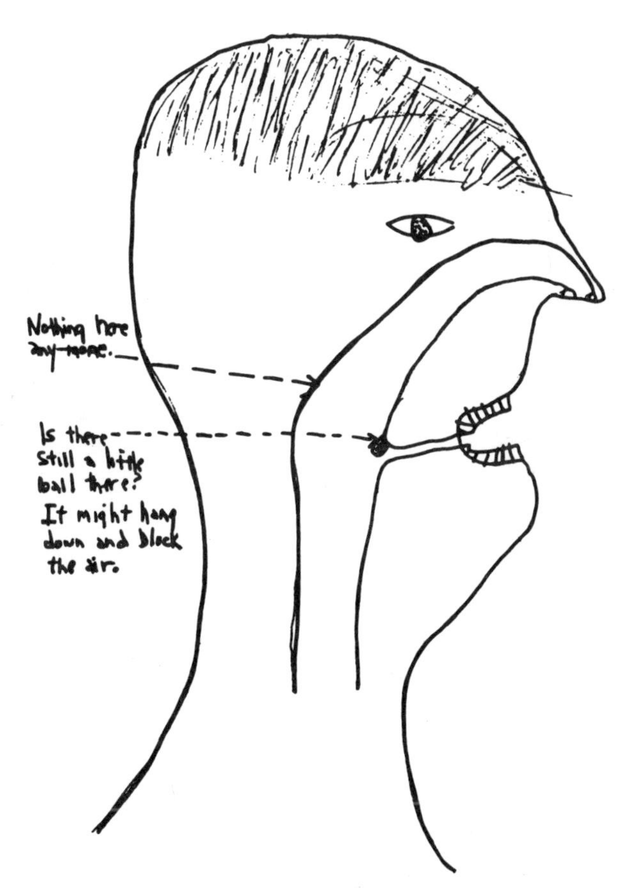

FIG. 4—"A GIRL." POSTOPERATIVE SKETCH BY 8-YEAR-OLD BOY.

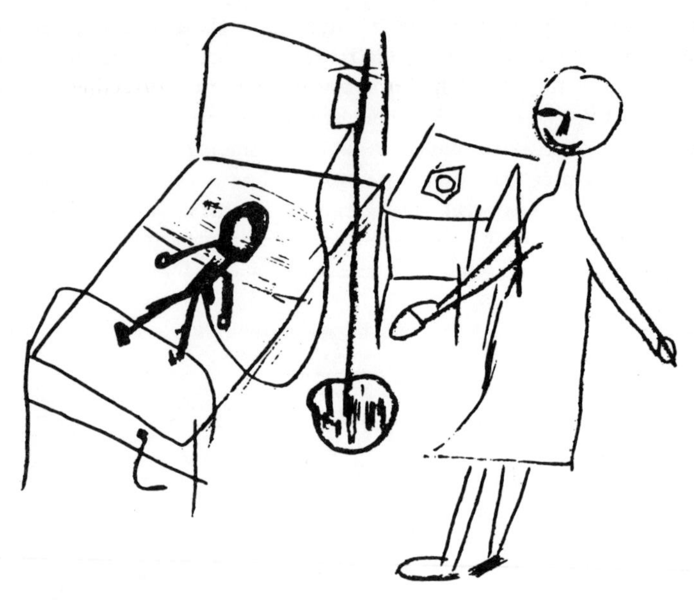

FIG. 5—DRAWING BY THERAPIST AT PATIENT'S DIRECTION, SHOWING BOY IN BED WITH PILLOW, SHEET, CRANK, BOTTLE, HOSE, STAND, SMILING NURSE, AND TABLE. NEEDLE LOCATION IS "BETWEEN BELLY AND ARM."

FIG. 6—DRAWING BY THERAPIST AT PATIENT'S DIRECTION, SHOWING I.V. NEEDLE IN GENITALS. THE BOY IS CRYING.

With Everett's permission, this version of his hospital experience was reviewed with his mother while the child listened and participated. Thus the mother and therapist together were involved in "correcting" the distorted memory.

After his mother was excused from the playroom, Everett and therapist discussed how little boys are often afraid when they go to the hospital, and especially that something scary will happen between their legs where the "wee-wee" comes out. Even though the nurse didn't really put the shot there, the child might be afraid she did, and then he would be afraid of little hoses later because they remind him of the way it was in the hospital. The therapist and patient discussed how a boy would feel if he could leave the hospital without being afraid anymore. The therapist was instructed to draw a happy boy, smiling and wearing a hat while going home from the hospital (see Fig. 7).

This child made a good recovery from his fear of darkness and hoses, and overcame his social withdrawal within a few weeks.

FIG. 7—"GOING HOME." DRAWING BY THERAPIST AT PATIENT'S DIRECTION, SHOWING A SMILE AND A HAT.

When a Child is Dying

Psychological Help for Dying Children

Rather than describe further what has been well-documented about sick children in other works (a good example of being Bergmann and Freud's *Children In the Hospital,* 1965), this section will try to extract some general principles from a dire situation: terminal illness. This area is poorly documented, despite the clear needs of many dying children for assistance with their emotional burdens. The lack of data may be attributed partly to the almost unbearable quality of adult experience when confronted by a dying child, which places severe limitations on psychological investigation.

Listening to Ravel's *Pavanne for a Dead Infant* allows one to feel a manageable dose of the painful emotions which the event of premature death brings to those who participate. Poets, including Wordsworth and Goethe, have struggled with the theme, sometimes with marked efforts to deny the reality of a child's death. Rückert, a poet of nineteenth-century Germany, wrote a series of over four hundred poems, entitled *Kindertotenlieder,* in response to the death of his own two youngsters. Planck's translation of one of that extraordinary series conveys the need of an adult to postpone and negate the awesome truth:*

> The Servant comes to tell the children
> Their sister has died. They hear it said,
> And yet with one voice say the brothers:
> It is not true, she is not dead.
>
> They see her white, they see her lying,
> Her lip so pale that was so red,
> And whisper softly as replying:
> It is not true, she is not dead.
>
> They see the mother weeping, waning,
> The father's tears his heart has bled,
> And yet their chorus is remaining:
> It is not true, she is not dead.
>
> And when the day came and the hours
> To lay her in her final bed,
> To lower her beneath the flowers:
> It is not true, she is not dead.

---

* Planck, Emma: Medical Times, Vol. 92, No. 7, 1964, p. 639.

May she remain your sister longer,
May every year her beauty spread
And may your love grow ever stronger—
It is not true, she is not dead.

The difficulties of adult investigators and therapists in dealing with dying children are not made any easier by the children themselves. Childhood communications about death in general are understandably faulty. Young children, when faced by the death of another person, especially a parent or sibling, usually find it difficult to express openly their sad feelings. Such expressions are often momentary and small in quantity compared to adult outpourings. Children are thus often thought to be lacking in feeling, although careful investigation reveals that their emotions are profound and often more fatefully long-lasting than those of more quickly-mourning adults. This expressive difficulty must be considered when thinking of children's emotions in the face of their own impending death. Much may be underground, waiting for the careful listener to hear.

Further, children's intellectual comprehension of death is quite faulty throughout the first ten (or more) years of life. It would be desirable, but beyond the limits of this presentation, to do more than mention the findings of Piaget and Nagy about the developmental features of healthy children's understanding of death. Briefly, it has been fairly well-established that preschoolers have little understanding of the finality of death. No matter how clearly informed, they still regard death as reversible. There is a strong tendency for children up to age five to believe life is equated with movement. Soon thereafter a tendency develops to personify death as a malevolent person who pursues the living (Piaget, 1928; Nagy, 1948). Obstacles to comprehension are similar to those parents find when trying to inform children how a seed is planted inside the mother's womb. Simultaneous or alternating with an understanding of the process as taught, preschoolers maintain their phase-appropriate and individually varying fantasies of oral and anal impregnation.

In reviewing Eissler's work, *The Psychiatrist and the Dying Patient* (1955), no reference to a dying child could be found. Indeed the relevant literature is quite sparse. This is especially true of investigations conducted in an unstructured manner, giving opportunity for fatally ill children to express their fantasies and knowledge. Such investigations are almost completely lacking. Even where an effort to listen to a child was made, skilled and thoughtful therapists such as Emma Planck tended to approach the child's statements with preconceived ideas and prohibition of full communication. In presenting a case, Planck (1964) injects the thought: "Life but not death is children's business. When a child who may conceivably die during hospitalization brings up the question of the possibility of his own death, we reassure him with great conviction and help him to deny the possibility. We would not reconcile the child with thoughts of his own death or feel a need to prepare him for it." [Bergmann (1965) indicates the same tendency.]

The child about whom Planck's preliminary remarks were made was later described playing with a doll who is fantasied to be sick. "She's got to stay in bed and get an I.V., and then she can get up and play. . . . She's not gonna die . . . ." Reviewing the description it seems likely that the little girl was occupied with thoughts that the female doll, representing herself, was going to die. The child was in need of communication with an adult in some child-appropriate way about her fear that she would die. She was apparently not given an opportunity to share such fears.

Friedman and Chodoff (1963) state: "Some acknowlegment of the illness is often helpful, especially in the older child, in preventing the child from feeling isolated, believing that others are not aware of what he is experiencing, or feeling that his disease is 'too awful' to talk about."

Vernick and Karon at the National Cancer Institute have done an extensive study of 150 children, ranging in age from three to twenty years (1965). Results have been published only on the first fifty of these children. Personal communication from Vernick gives an impression that, even with the youngest children, as soon as the physician gives the news of a diagnosis of leukemia, a child immediately "knows" he has something very serious. His entire environment changes. The child quickly notices that the people whom he had previously trusted and loved are now keeping something frightening from him. Their silence is as if they were saying, "Please don't ask me about this for it is too terrible."

A nine-year-old girl in Vernick's care remarked, "I knew it was leukemia. I knew I had something serious and leukemia is serious." An eleven-year-old said, "I know there is no cure for leukemia. But at least I'm glad you told me what I have." A sixteen-year-old who was not told the diagnosis by his mother for six months until twelve hours before his death, lamented, "Mother, I knew I had it all along." He had, in effect, been out of forthright communication with her for half a year.

Vernick and Karon have repeatedly noted that failure to discuss the diagnosis with the child contributes to behavior problems. The patient may be told the diagnosis and other truths by strangers and especially neighborhood children. Vernick believes the best way to strengthen the child against "the thoughtless barbs of his peer group" is to discuss the diagnosis with him beforehand.

An illustration of the practical value of Vernick's hospital work is the case of a ten-year-old who was uncooperative on admission, frightened, withdrawn, whining, crying, refusing medication. He revealed he did not know his diagnosis but, while in the office of his family doctor, his parents were called and he was left alone. He knew nothing of what they had been told, but knew his parents had some knowledge not shared with him, about which he was worried. When the medical staff guided his parents to discuss "the great mystery surrounding his hospitalization," his parents gave the doctor permission to speak to the child about his diagnosis. The patient became more open, cheerful, relaxed, and problems about refusing medications practically disappeared. Other children on the ward noticed this change and called it amazing.

Among other findings of the National Cancer Institute group is that children often will not ask questions of the staff or their parents. Instead they wait for adults to show a readiness to anticipate and deal with their serious concerns. Only then will they reveal the pre-existing worry. Vernick and Karon also caution that the child who is gravely ill is "worrying about dying and is eager to have someone help him talk about it. If he is passive, it may only be a reflection of how little the environment helps him to express his concerns." A nine-year-old girl described how frightened she was when nobody talked to her about her downhill course: "It was like they were getting ready for me to die."

Studying "Death Anxiety in Children with a Fatal Illness," James Morrissey (1964) reports on fifty children, sixteen of whom he judged to be aware or suspicious of the fatal nature of their illness. A three-and-one-half-year-old child had considerable anxiety about her own death. (She and another child, to be mentioned later, are the only fatally ill preschoolers about whom detailed psychological observations have been found in the literature). Shortly after the onset of her lymphocytic leukemia she remarked that "Jesus" was "coming down from Heaven" to take her there. She wondered if Jesus had toys in heaven. She seemed quite worried and upset that she would die, and did not want to go to heaven. Instead she wanted to stay at home and be with her mother. On one occasion while being prepared for sleep she asked, "Am I going to die?" and added, "You know, God is going to come down from heaven and God is going to take me back with Him."

Solnit (1963) believes it has become apparent "that a more systematic investigation of a child's psychological reactions to his own dying will have to take into account the adults' tendency not to perceive the dying child's behavioral and verbal communications about his own fears because of the anxiety evoked in the adult by the dying child." With this open-eared approach, among the cases they describe is one of four-year-old Larry, who was aware of his impending death. Larry was dying from a widely metastasized neuroblastoma. He became quite attached to a young intern caring for him. Once in a panic before the induction of anesthesia for a diagnostic operation, Larry asked the intern to sing a certain lullaby which his mother always sang before she tucked him in. His relationship to the doctor grew and Larry confided more. On the day before Larry died, he asked the intern to hold him and said he was afraid to die. His doctor should "promise to come anytime" Larry "needed" him. The intern was amazed, and wondered for how long Larry had known of his impending death. The next day, when the child died in a coma, his parents reassured themselves by saying that Larry had never known he was dying. The authors quote several other children as having even more clear awareness of their impending death, far beyond that acknowledged by their parents and physicians.

CASE REPORT: A Fatally Ill Boy in Analysis at Age Four: Charles

A psychoanalytic approach can provide a clear view of a dying child's fantasies and concerns, as well as information regarding the extent of his realistic appraisal of his physical situation. The rare opportunity to gain such understanding was presented by the attendance of a leukemic child at a therapeutic nursery school (The Cornerstone School, in which analysis is conducted in the classroom setting). The first two-months work of that study will be described here, as it reveals some general principles useful in management of a fatally ill preschooler.

Charles was four years and seven months old when he entered nursery school and began analysis simultaneously. His leukemia had been diagnosed seven months previously, close to his fourth birthday. Having been hospitalized for two weeks, during which he received a sternal puncture, blood transfusion, and numerous finger punctures, Charles emerged from the hospital with daytime urinary incontinence, occasional soiling, marked whining and clinging. All of these were new troubles, although he had previously been incontinent of urine at night—a behavior which continued after hospitalization. Charles slept in his mother's bedroom (in a separate bed) for two weeks after coming home. When he enrolled in a regular nursery-school program, he was unable to separate from his mother in order to attend and grew worse in regard to both enuresis and daytime urinary incontinence. His play activities tended to be more and more with girls, less and less with boys, and generally confined to playing house. He would usually be the baby or the mother, and wore mostly girls' clothes during such play. His mother complained that he was becoming increasingly "identified" with herself and his sisters in mannerisms and speech. Alert, charming, and always playful, Charles was especially interested in music. His "cultural" activities continued to progress during the seven months of known leukemic disease. He picked out tunes on the piano, had good pitch in his frequent singing, spoke in a coy, girlish way with a precocious vocabulary, painted and drew with advanced levels of skill.

Charles's leukemia was by no means the only burden in his early life. His sisters (two and four years older) and he witnessed many quarrels between their parents. From the time he was two years and six months old until he was four years old, there was almost no period of marital harmony. After several separations and reconciliations, permanent separation of the parents occurred when Charles was three, followed by a divorce—completed only two weeks before the diagnosis of leukemia was made—near his fourth birthday.

In view of the context of this report, it should be pointed out that Charles had apparently experienced deprivation of paternal affection, certainly beginning no later than age two. Not only was paternal presence lacking, but it became clear that, during increasingly infrequent weekend visits to his children, the father began to show a marked preference for the company of his daughters. Charles complained of this experience for a few months, but by age four had stopped complaining. Paternal attention diminished more conspicuously following the divorce and then the diagnosis of leukemia. Charles's mother reported the father moved to another city. He was unwilling to come in for medical conferences following the onset of weakness and anemia which precipitated Charle's hospitalization. When psychoanalysis began seven months later, the father made frequent trips to the local area but never accepted the analyst's requests for conferences regarding his son.

Charles's father was known to us mainly through his mother. She described him as an emotionally detached, intellectually absorbed executive. Charles's description of his father centered about a pattern of his father first inviting Charles to come along and then playing tennis with adults while Charles grew impatient and finally wandered off by himself.

Throughout the experience of his parents' quarrels, separation and divorce, Charles received no direct communication of the reasons for the marital difficulty. Unclarity and incompleteness was also the analyst's experience when trying to gain understanding of the marital circumstances which preceded the divorce.

Charles's mother presented herself to the analyst as a sad, weary, harassed young woman who found it impossible to honor appointments at all, or else could not arrive on time for the first few months. She spent much time complaining of the mechanical disrepair of her automobile, and derived numerous gallows-humor examples from "the contraption" and its hazards. A graduate of a fine college, after Charles became ill she took a medical technician's course. She hoped to contribute to research in leukemia through this latter endeavor. Her oldest child began to steal a few days after being given a rather ambiguous explanation of Charles's illness and received prompt brief psychotherapy with a rapid favorable response.

Family history of relevance includes the death of the mother's sister when the mother was fifteen. The sister was about four years old at the time (approximately Charles's age). A peculiar feature is that the mother recalls that her sister's death was due to "osteomyelitis associated with a very high white count." (There is a form of leukemia which sometimes becomes manifest as an osteomyelitis.) The osteomyelitis was of one leg. One of the first manifestations of Charles's leukemia was a complaint of fatigue with leg pain. Particularly while walking upstairs, he would say, "My legs hurt too much to walk." (The mother looks back ruefully to those early days of his illness—when she tended to underestimate his complaints.) Perhaps a residue of her own sibling bereavement inhibited her response to Charles's leg pains.

Initial examination. Charles was quite friendly, overly ingratiating, and surprisingly spontaneous in discussing his hospitalization— which had taken place over half a year prior to the first interview. His first mention of his illness was in connection with my being a doctor, and his having been in a hospital where he "had a wonderful time and watched a lot of TV." After discussing the supposed "good time" and helping Charles with his efforts to draw some of the TV characters he had in mind, I pointed out that what he said was a kind of "opposite talk." He readily agreed that it hadn't all "been a good time. Just some of it was a good time."

Not only was a denial of the painful and fearful experience involved, but also a reversal of affect—recounting memories of events and affects as if they were a story about "Mickey Mouse from TV." At the child's request I started to draw Mickey Mouse and he finished it. I only drew the outline of the head and he filled it in. This drawing was a complicated communication. Mickey Mouse had some extra fingers and Charles made a very distinct effort to be sure that I put in an extra foot for Mickey. This was very important to him. I tried to resist for a minute, frustrating the effort by asking what this was about. Charles wouldn't be frustrated. Mickey Mouse had to have a third foot at once (see Fig. 8). I interpreted to him that a child might make this kind of drawing if he had a sickness that he was worried about. The child might feel it would be very good to have some extra parts around in case he might have some trouble with his body and might need those extra parts. I was impressed with how ready Charles was to accept this kind of talk.

Following two individual sessions, Charles entered a classroom group with three other children. All were in analysis in the classroom setting, for six hours a week. Two teachers assisted and provided regular nursery-school activities. (For details of this method, which is of value for preventive as well as therapeutic work, see Kliman, 1966.)

Work with Charles's mother. It soon became apparent that certain parallels of distortion existed in the views of both mother and child of facts in their daily life. An example arose when Charles told me the name of his summer-school teacher. It wasn't really his teacher's name that he gave me. His real teacher was an entirely different woman. When I asked the mother for permission to speak to his summer-school teacher, the mother gave me the same wrong name. It turned out that both child and mother had wanted to have that "wrong-named" teacher and were very disappointed when they got another who was not so much in tune with their personalities.

Charles revealed another distortion when he insisted that his pediatrician, whom he had been seeing every few weeks for seven months, was his sister's doctor. In a multiply-determined distortion of reality, Charles once more preferred to be female. His distortion equated him with one of his lively, healthy sisters who would outlive him and also

FIG. 8—A MICKEY MOUSE WITH EXTRA PARTS. PSYCHOLOGICAL EMERGENCY: A BOY WITH LEUKEMIA AT AGE FOUR. (DRAWN ORIGINALLY IN SEVEN COLORS OF CRAYON ON A SHEET OF PAPER 8½ x 11 INCHES.)

avoided the unpleasant doctor who gives him bad news and pain. (Similarly, the teacher whom he didn't want to have for a teacher would not "be" his teacher. Let the nice one be his teacher.)

In early months of analysis an effort was made to undo some distortions, choosing them because they were not in themselves vital to the child's psychological economy. Approaching from the periphery, the distortions were used as examples to test the possibility that Charles could make a better adaptation by sharing the realities than by sharing adult avoidances of realities. Gradually his mother was helped to undo some distortions, beginning with the teacher's name. Then we began to talk with his mother about her avoidance of discussing with Charles some of the grim facts in his life. At that point, Charles began to spontaneously refer to his doctor appropriately.

Our educational director, Mrs. Doris Gorin, who was the head teacher of Charles's class, had the responsibility of conducting weekly guidance sessions with Charles's mother and three other mothers of children then in the small class. (The analyst sees each family once a month.) We began gently to ask Charles's mother what it was like from the boy's point of view to go to the doctor and to the hospital for frequent tests, to be in a hospital, to take medicine every day, and not to have one thing said about why he was taking the medicine, why he was getting the tests, why he had been in the hospital, why he had a blood transfusion or why he had a painful puncture of his breastbone. Charles's mother gradually began to see that it was really burdensome to her child to have no explanation of these procedures. She re-entered therapy herself and learned that her avoidance of communication had some relationship to her previous experience of the death of her sister. Her work on the crisis in Charles's illness appeared to have some value in reorganizing her attitude toward the previous adaptive crisis.

We began guiding Charles's mother on the subject of other current illnesses in her family. Her own mother was then seriously ill. Another grandparent was dying. We suggested that these somewhat more distant illnesses might be used by some children to initiate discussions about sickness and death, feelings about death, and fears about death.

Staff attitudes. We soon came to be very sympathetic with the mother's difficulties. Unlike Charles's mother, we did not often avoid issues. However, the analyst found himself suffering from a small amnesia about some of the data at one point. One of our staff members was in tears on first learning the child's diagnosis. The educational director discovered and reported to me that she found herself in a mild, but still uncharacteristic, deviousness with this little boy. She had gone to the child's home for the home visit (a procedure always done prior to the opening of class) and said to him—knowing full well that both of his sisters were in school —"Where are your sisters today?" Consciously she felt she was trying to make conversation. But upon reflection she reported the conversation in her daily supervisory conference with me, so that I could discuss it with her. It was an avoidance of knowledge. The child had known that she knew where the sisters were. She took it up with Charles at the first opportunity. We let the mother know about some of our difficulties and shared some of our own pain with her so she would not feel alone.

One day Charles told me that he had an ache in his eye. Another day this same eye ached him. Meanwhile, he had a facial rash which evoked in me a fantasy of leukemic invasion of his skin. A difficulty then occurred. I was supervising the educational director and on the previous day had given her a lengthy account of my analytic work with Charles so that she would be up to date. I said, "There's something else I want to tell you but I just can't think what it is except that I know it's important. It will come to me in a while, but how did you get that mark on your eye?" She told me about her eye, but I still didn't remember that I was worried about Charles's eye-ache and the rash on his face. It was only when I went back in to the schoolroom and saw Charles's face that my associations began to flow.

We learned that the mother had told all the other families on the street about Charles's leukemia. One of the other parents in the school came in one day and said, "I understand Charles is in hemotologic or clinical remission." He said this in Charles's presence. During an interview concerning Charles's siblings,* his mother made a slip about a dog that had died—a dog which had already become a focus in our interest. She explained, as she had to the head teacher, that she couldn't bear to tell the children of the death of this dog which had occurred now a week before. Then she said, "The day *Charles* died, I just couldn't bear to tell the children that they had suffered another loss." She became aware of her slip spontaneously.

The first two months of analysis. These early months are described in detail because they contain work which was particularly related to Charles's latest psychological emergencies: his fatal illness and geographic separation from his father. One of Charles's first communications to me in the classroom was a communication about pleasurable aggression against himself. "I just love to hit my own thumb!" Charles then gave some hints of connections between his feminine identity and his stay in the hospital. He pretended to be Cinderella and dressed up as a girl,

* Conducted by Mrs. Ann Kliman as part of the Center's study of family crises.

saying, "I watched that in the hospital." He began to invent deviously aggressive methods of getting even with other children in the class when they hit him or were mean. He wouldn't hit back, but would say, "I'm going to get even with you. I'm going to give you a present that'll be the worst present you ever had!" "You like trucks," he said to one child at whom he was angry. "I'm going to give you one, but it'll be so rusty you can't play with it." To another: "You like dolls—I'm going to give you one that's no good.

About the middle of the first month of analysis he indicated some hopes for the future. No doubt they were denials, but also some evidence of what might be phallic strivings such as, "When I grow up I'm going to have a car." (A few months later he was going to be a jet pilot.) But he now spoke of being scared by TV shows, about being lost in space, and about one-eyed robots. Perhaps his distress about one-eyed robots was a way of telling us of his fears about his eyes which ached very much. He began to try to master these fears in a forthright fashion. He took some plasticene (his own facial skin bespeckled with an alarming-looking rash) and made a mold of the teacher's hand, saying, "This (clay) is skin. I'm a doctor. I'm going to fiind out what's the matter with the skin." He took a knife, like a good pathologist, sliced the skin, studied a section, held it up, and very slowly gave his opinion, "It's going to be all right." He put it down and went about other play activities. He soon began to be open about more intimate expressions of curiosity and fantasy. "Teacher doesn't have any underwear." While he was on the floor, he tried to look up the teacher's skirt and said, "I can see her behind."

In the third week of analysis Charles fantasied little lost lambs, lonely, in need of protection. He brought some toy lambs into a block shelter, built a great fortress around them, and when it was all closed up he said, "You have to be careful to leave some windows open because they can die from no air." This was his first analytic expression of fear about death. He explained that people can die from no air, too, ". . . but in my house it's all right to have all the windows shut. We have water, and from the water we get air when the water dries up. So we can always breathe."

At this point came a dramatic turn in Charles's analysis and in his clinical progress. His mother had decided to "level" with her children ten days after the death of the dog. By now Charles had been well-established in analysis, and had made the communications already described. Five minutes before class started, his mother chose to tell him about the dog. Upon entering class behind his mother, he came to me. Then he sat down and had his mother sit next to me in the nursery school room. Very seriously, and with appropriate sadness he said, "You know, Spot was sick and he died." Then he added, "You know, I'm sick and I'm going to die." This was said with calm sadness.

Despite and because of the work I had done with Charles up to that point, this was a distressing communication which evoked sadness and anxiety in me. Perhaps it was helpful to the child to feel my distress and particularly my sadness. Perhaps one has to be prepared to die a little with the patient, as Eissler advises.

I drew him out about his illness and the dog's death. Step by step I shared with him my serious views and elicited from him his serious views. I agreed with him, "Yes," that "Spot had died, and that it was a serious sickness that must have made Spot die. But wasn't his serious sickness a different matter?" . . . "Spot's a dog nobody knew was sick and you're a child whose family knows he is sick. . . . Spot never even went to a dog doctor or hospital, and nobody even knew that Spot was sick. Nobody could help Spot. Spot never got dog medicine, never got dog blood, didn't take dog pills every day, like you do—even two different kinds. They didn't take dog blood tests every two weeks. It's different for you even though you do have a serious sickness and you might die from it, because children do die from the serious sickness you have. . . ." This statement of his possible death did not remove Charles's attention to me.

My lengthy response was a "dose" of reality. It was a pediatric dose of bitter truth contained in a sweetened syrup of hope. It seemed appropriate to the child's developmental status and intellectual abilities.

Charles proceeded well in his analysis. He persistently used the telephone to communicate with me. Much discussion and fantasy emerged about how to fix things, such as kitchen parts. He wanted to make a magic stove with a button which, if pressed, would fix all the other parts of the stove so it would never break again. He expressed denial and hopefulness in this omnipotent fixer-button fantasy, which I was able to interpret as related to his wish that he could get well forever by being fixed in a magic way. I supported this wish by saying, "Wouldn't it be wonderful if you could?" I never said to him, "Charles, you'll never get well."

A difficult time arose when another child's father died quite unexpectedly in a car crash. This child was in Charles's class. The complexities of that experience were enormous, but included Charles's desire to avoid coming to class and analysis. This was dealt with by permitting him to come but not forcing him to speak about whatever he didn't wish to speak about. Nevertheless, he managed to speak somewhat about the dead father. Following the discussion about the dead father he put on a cloth and called it a skirt, indicating his use of feminine identification as a defense against massive anxiety. He then disclosed a fantasy that his mother had a husband who had died, and he had a father who was divorced.

Charles was quite an original child. Among his original songs were: "If I were an orange I'd eat me," and "If I were a tooth I'd scrunch me." He was still quite orally occupied in many ways, but it was remarkable that in the midst of his fear and conscious knowledge about his own impending death, he was able to deal somewhat with his oedipal problems and sexual confusions. He told me about a bull. The bull was called "daddy cow" and had a baby cow inside which gets born. The daddy and baby cow get lassoed by a cowboy. The daddy cow gets squeezed so hard that he dies, but the baby cow lives still inside the daddy. Later the daddy cow comes back to life. The dying and coming back to life are repeated several times. Then came a story of a boy who got so angry at his daddy that he tried to kill the daddy. Why? Because the daddy kissed the mommy!

The story carries a communication about the reversibility of death, which any child his age might believe. There is also a linkage between that reversibility of death and the reversibility of sexual roles—daddy cow being pregnant and giving birth. After these linked confusions were pointed out to him, Charles came out with a positive oedipal triangular story in which he, in a fit of jealousy, kills the father. This, again, indicated more strength than I had anticipated in this dying child. The underestimation stemmed from my own denial of the dying child's strength, suggesting a reason why therapists avoid the treatment as well as investigation of such children's psychological processes.

During the second month of analysis Charles proceeded with stories about how a parent deceives a child in a hospital by telling him that the food will be good when it is really terrible. By now the analytic and therapeutic relationships to myself and the teachers were so firm that at Thanksgiving time he said, "Damn, I wish there weren't any turkeys. I don't want to have Thanksgiving with no school." Analysts and teachers alike are accustomed to denial and reversal of emotional response at such times, as children try to convince themselves and adults of cheerfulness or brazenness rather than sadness at the moment of departure.

During the first two months of analysis, Charles revealed he shared with other four- and five-year-olds the idea that a dead person cannot move and cannot breathe. But being so attached to school and his analyst, he added an idiosyncratic detail about death: "A dead person can't breathe and can't move, but he can learn." This detail apparently signified that Charles wished to continue being with his teachers and analyst even when he was dead.

Blindness soon was mentioned by Charles as if it were equated with death. "Blind people are dead, even though they can move." For Charles, some of the separation problems of death and blindness were similar: not being able to see people whom he loved. Now that he was lonely for his dead dog, Spot, Charles drew pictures of him, saying, "I wish you could *see* Spot's face. It's so nice."

Varieties of oedipal fantasies came forth more and more in Charles's analytic material. He would drive a car for the purpose of saving his mother. He would take the wheel when she had an accident. He would save her. He would fly an airplane. He would swoop down from his jet airplane, pick up the damaged car, repair it, return it for mother to use.

By the end of his second month, Charles's clinical progress was definite. He no longer wet his bed at night, nor dampened his pants in the day. He did not soil any more. He separated readily from his mother, came to school willingly and went freely outdoors to play with friends after school. He played well with other children, was as creative as ever, and eager to learn from the books his mother and teachers read to him at his request.

Charles was overheard speaking to his classmates occasionally about his illness, and defined for them one aspect of its effect on his life: "I have a sickness, but it's the kind where I can go to school most of the time." He did not speak to the children about dying, but spoke of it to the analyst when other children could hear.

Charles was now open about certain resentments. "Why should I have to go to take blood tests every two weeks? My sisters don't have to go except once in a while." He hit his sisters when they were mean to him. He hit his mother a great deal, rather unprecedentedly, but under circumstances which the mother felt were justifying. He hit other children in the class when annoyed or hurt by them, a contrast to his intellectual revenges of the first month. Occasionally he would give the analyst a moderate blow, either in a jealous moment or as an act of defiance directed against the teachers as well as the analyst. He would occasionally knock over classroom equipment when angry, and—interesting in view of his thoughts about blindness and death—would pull down window shades and turn out lights in bursts of mischievous glee.

Ever-continuing occupation with deterioration of his body was suggested by Charles's response while watching another child punch holes in a paper cup. "That's like punching holes in skin. If you really did that to a person, they would bleed. The blood would come out of the holes." He stopped, thought, got very tense, saying, "Then the bones would come out, and then the eyes would come out, and then the person would die."

Medical evaluation of Charles's physical status in the first two months of analysis. Charles was under the regular care of a pediatrician and hematologist, who—like his therapists at school—worked to some extent as a coordinated team. They reported Charles to be in good hematologic remission, with no evidence of active disease during this period. He was judged capable of participating fully in all physical activities. His medication consisted of two forms of antimitotic agents, given in series. Two weeks with one agent were followed by two weeks with the other agent. His facial rash was possibly allergic but never well-understood. Occasional anorexia and nausea were thought to be effects of one antimitotic agent, but in time was noted to appear while the other was being received.

Physical prognosis could not be given in a definitive fashion, the pediatrician and hematologist advised. Some children had been known to live as long as five years with remissions and exacerbations of leukemia treated by the methods which were being applied in Charles's case. The mean life expectancy was one year, of which nine months had passed at this point. With passage of each month there was statistical reason to expect survival even longer than one year, but no special criteria could be applied for such predictions in any given child.

Discussion of the first two months' material. By the end of the first two months time the analyst and, through him, the child's teachers and mother, had confronted Charles with a multidirectional effort to correct and compensate for his multiple pathogenic experiences. *The pathogenic deprivations, in themselves multiple, had been approached as follows:*

1. Deprivation of emotional investment from the mother was partly corrected by helping the mother overcome her avoidance of communication with the dying child. This reduced a major obstacle to healthy "influx" of emotional supplies.
2. Deprivation of paternal affection and investment was partly corrected by establishing an intense relationship with an adult male, the analyst, who was with the child six hours each week in the classroom.
3. Deprivation of emotional experience with heterosexual "teams" of adults was partly corrected by the establishment of intense relationships with the analyst-teachers team.

Charles's experience with sensations of weakness, fatigue, subtle experiences of body-image change, and perception of painful medical procedures all were part of a "fear experience." That fear experience was potentially, if not actually, pathogenic, compounded, as it was, by an absence of information from his parents concerning the purpose and meaning of what was being done to help him. *The fear experience was approached by:*

1. Helping the patient's mother to share with the child her own emotional resources in dealing with the realistic danger to him.
2. Offering the analyst as an object with whom the patient could share fears and discuss both the realistic danger and reverberations with *neurotic anxiety and conflicts related to Charles's fantasies and underlying problems.*

In some ways, Charles's thoughts about death were met much as a child's thoughts about sexual behavior could be met at this age in the midst of an analysis. The family was helped to deal with what the child observed or had already asked or spoken about—notably the death of his pet, about which his perceptions and feelings were presumably highly accessible. Just as it probably would not be useful to explain to a child of this age aspects of adult sexual activity which had not come to his attention, it was not considered desirable for the child to be confronted with aspects of his illness and the process of dying which would be incomprehensible and perplexing to him (provided there was no evidence that the child was already trying to cope with these aspects). It was considered essential as in sexual matters, that the patient should be allowed to know that death can occur at his age. He was brought back into the channel of communication on this matter, rather than separated from his mother, whose own emotional life was perceptibly reverberating with the knowledge of her child's impending death.

Vernick and Karon concluded their study of leukemic children in a hospital by asking, "Who's afraid of death in a leukemia ward?" They answered "Everyone." The resolution of that fear was everyone's problem on the ward. In an atmosphere of complete freedom for their child patients to express their concerns. Vernick and Karon found that most of the children already knew their illness, and some knew exactly what was wrong. Their staff was able to abandon traditional tactics of protecting children by being secretive, and as a consequence became actively and constructively involved in helping their patients cope with the realistic experience of fear. They reported marked diminution in withdrawal, depression and behavior disorder whch are so frequent on leukemia wards.

Up to this point, Charles's treatment has tended to confirm the findings of Vernick and Karon. Charles was capable of verbalizing his own incurability and impending death. His comprehension of these matters was appropriately immature and faulty, like his sexual ideas. He believed in the incompleteness and reversability of death in a way comparable to his belief in the ability of a bull to bear a baby cow. He appeared to feel much better when he communicated about his illness, fears and fantasies. His improvements were by no means simply the result of improved communication about illness and death. He was a paternally deprived child, and to some extent a maternally deprived child. Partial corrections of those deprivations had been distinctly helpful. Each relationship involved in such corrections had a common and basic feature. That feature was not only warmth, but a combination of warmth with persistent truthfulness and willingness to listen.

Emerging from Charles's analysis was a process which might be called "pediatric dosage of reality." As with all powerful medicines, there are a few patients who should never receive doses of certain realities for special reasons. As with all medicines, the smallest doses should be given the smallest children. The capactiy to usefully absorb is smaller and the toxic dose might be more easily exceeded in the exposure of young children to painful reality. The necessity for containing the pediatric dose within a suitable vehicle has become clear, and the desirable vehicle appears to be reliable human relationships in this case, including reliable medical care.

Also emerging from the analysis in the first two months were indications of special problems in the assisting adults. Not only Charles's mother and father, but also his analyst and teachers, were clearly distressed and to some extent conflicted about Charles's experiences. These distresses and conflicts tended to interfere with treatment of the child. Recognition of staff difficulties occurred early enough to permit greater empathy for the mother's experience, an empathy which supported her in dealing more responsively with the child's own experiences.

Illness of a Parent

Physical Illness

Just as the reactions of the human body to illness are legion, the reactions of children of different ages to the countless different illnesses of adults are also bewilderingly varied. Fortunately, careful history-taking, gathering facts from both the child and his parents, usually provides the clinician with sufficient leads for a working formulation of preventive and therapeutic value. It should be kept in mind that chronic illnesses of the parent are even more likely than acute (nonfatal) illnesses to provide an unmanageable burden to an immature psychological economy.

CASE REPORT

A mother had a rare form of multiple sclerosis, which had first appeared in her teens. Now at age 40 she had a 17-year-old son as well as two younger boys, three and five years his junior. By the time the 17-year-old, Harold, presented himself for psychotherapy he had already been examined by his internist, and even hospitalized for cystoscopy because of urinary symptoms which the internist ultimately concluded required psychotherapy rather than more physical investigation.

During his first interview, Harold obviously wanted help and presented an extraordinarily vivid account of his mental life. Yet it was not until a month later that it became known that his mother was covertly suffering from an outbreak of her chronic disease and was very frightened about increasing visual defects. A combination of medical attention for the mother and once-a-week psychotherapy for Harold proved very fruitful. An account of his brief therapy (30 sessions over a period of eight months) illustrates the surprising accessibility of illness-related material, with a partial correction of pathological identifications with aspects of his mother's illness.

In the initial interview Harold stated his complaint as ". . . a lot of nervousness, hard to sit still, fingers and feet restless all the time. My worst problem is at night when I have lots of tense fantasies about what will happen in school socially the next day. As I'm trying to fall asleep I feel my bladder getting full and I have to go to the bathroom a couple of times in a row, even on into the middle of the night." Harold's first interview is especially worthy of attention because his improvement began from that time. The work done during the first session suggests that even a very brief intervention may have been helpful to this particular boy. Nevertheless, he requested and was granted further treatment.

Harold described some of the nighttime fantasies, and told me that most of them centered about a group of boys of which he is the leader. "This group is a splinter-faction, cut off from the main stream of social life." His imagination takes him into fantasies of disputes between "the main stream" (a group which he really likes) and his own group. He gets tense in the midst of imaginary quarrels and then cannot fall asleep.

Urged to give details about the evolution of these nighttime fantasies, he described with remarkable clarity that a few years ago he would imagine himself being "a revolutionary general who led uprisings all over the world, to overthrow established governments." This before-sleep fantasy was so detailed that sometimes he would even decide "how many buttons there would be on the uniforms" of his revolutionary army.

Unaware of the likely connections between his "revolutionary" tendency and his next thought, Harold explained that he is much less tense when away from home. His parents would not let him watch TV freely, discouraged him from having friends in the house, and insisted that he "must only study, study, study."

After having given all the above information spontaneously, Harold was asked if there were any other circumstances in the house which might be causing him tension. He readily brought out: "My mother has a disease which might cripple her or kill her, only I don't think it will. She has multiple sclerosis, supposedly since her teens. Now at age 40 she is making medical history by being improved. She has a leg go bad or an eye go bad now and then. She has lots of automobile accidents . . . some of them very serious, nearly fatal, wrecking the car. . . ." Harold did not connect these accidents with the mother's multiple sclerosis. When specifically asked if the mother had any difficulty with bladder control, he completely denied that any such problem existed. It seemed clear that Harold had a strong need to deny his mother's illness in certain ways. He would admit that it was serious and possibly fatal, just as he would admit the seriousness and near fatality of her automobile accidents. Yet he had to isolate the two sets of facts and deny that the visual difficulties and leg-use problem, which he knew about, had any connection with the driving problems. By noticing in himself the horror aroused by contemplating Harold's mother partly paralyzed and partly driving a car and imagining the dreadful hazard to herself and others on the highway, the therapist began to appreciate how great a task it must be for Harold to deal with his family's grim realities.

Rather than challenge Harold's defensive denial immediately, it was decided to continue the process of history-taking in the hope of encouraging catharsis and self-observation as a preliminary to better reality-testing and ultimately interpretation of the connection between his bladder trouble and the presumably defended-against knowledge of his mother's comparable physical problem.

As an encouraging apparent result of this on-the-spot decision not to challenge his defenses, but rather to encourage expressivity, Harold continued by adding rather casually, "Two years ago my father was told not to eat high-cholesterol foods because they might kill him. He was getting chest pains and had a very high-cholesterol count. There was some trouble on the cardiogram. Now everything is fine except he might drop dead at any time. The whole family has a kind of morbid humor on this subject, a devil-may-care, live and enjoy life while you can attitude." Doing nothing more than making a mental note to learn from the parents the facts of the father's and mother's illnesses the therapist waited. Harold appeared to shift the subject to his younger brother who has psychological problems "which I don't feel like going into right now."

The therapist then returned to the parental-illnesses and made a statement that this amount of potentially fatal physical illness in one family was a powerful cause of tension. To this, Harold responded by reporting a dream he had had the night before: "I was walking along a steep ledge near a lake. Other kids were running happily along the ledge, jumping from one rock to another. But I was just crawling along, scared stiff, afraid I would fall into the water."

Asked to tell what the various parts of the dream brought to mind, Harold said that nothing special was coming to mind except the good times other kids have and how he is different because he is cooped up by his parents. He quickly recognized when it was pointed out that there was a representation of other children's happiness in the dream—their happily skipping from stone to stone. Asked what he thought about his being unable to move (scared stiff) he was reminded of a feeling he "once had in an airplane in a storm. I was so frightened that I tried to hypnotize myself into getting calm. Oh, about that lake, I'm realizing that there's a lot of water in my thoughts. I have lots of dreams about water." Shortly thereafter it was pointed out to him that he had used a water image in regard to the "main stream" of school life, and that possibly this was a clue to his urinary problem. Harold added: his terrible fear in the airplane was that it would fall into the ocean; when nervous he gets a lack of water in his mouth and throat; in a way this mouth dryness is about water because it is the opposite of wetness.

Next Harold's parents were interviewed, who added to his history that Harold was disinterested in learning to drive. They had believed his urinary difficulties were physical in origin, but during the session not only were they able to give up this position but they also spontaneously came up with the idea that Harold's unusual disinterest in driving might be connected with the bad experiences his mother had had in automobile accidents. It was decided in this case that the emphasis would be on direct treatment of the child with occasional conferences with the parents. A once-a-week schedule for him and once-a-month for the parents was agreed upon and carried out for eight months.

A major feature of the work was a focus on Harold's driving inhibition. He was eager to attribute it to his disgust about promiscuous children, and a fear that if he drove he might be like some of his friends who are very loose sexually. It was with much greater difficulty that he realized that he was behaving as if he were his mother. If he were his mother, then, and only then, would it be realistic for him to be so unusually afraid of driving. He was impressed by this interpretation and a few weeks later made some efforts to learn to drive. However, the main effect apparently was to lead him into greater concentration on the need to face the importance of his mother's illness in his life.

During a week when his mother had an exacerbation of her visual defects, Harold reported a dream of beating up his mother. In association with his dream he revealed a desire to beat up many people who have insulted or injured him, despite a conscious opposition to any actual physical violence.

The relationship between his mother's newly increased weakness and the dream about beating her up was further clarified by some complaining associations. Harold felt somewhat more needy than usual and worried as well as resentful about possible deprivations his mother's increased weakness might impose upon him. An additional determinant of his violence in the dream was brought out by the therapist: that when another person is rather helpless, she cannot be relied on to control one's own violent impulses. Harold's mother could not be counted on to restrain her adolescent son, who had increasing physical domination over her as he grew stronger and she grew weaker.

In retrospect, the treatment seemed successful for one of such brevity. His urinary problems cleared up nearly to the point of being negligible. He spoke realistically of his mother's illness and his associated anxieties. His yearning for a healthier mother emerged, as well as dreads of losing his own mother by her death. He was instrumental in clarifying the neurotic nature of his father's supposed heart ailment, to his own relief. His social life expanded moderately, not without discomfort. He began to drive, although with readily discerned conflict. He made plans to attend college away from home and looked forward not only to the increased freedom the college situation would provide, but also to a chance to live somewhat free from his family's tensions.

Relatively untouched in this particular case was Harold's sense of guilt about his mother's helplessness, and about his consequent power over her. He gave some hints that sexual strivings for her were closer to consciousness than in most boys his age toward their mothers. For more data on the genesis of guilty reactions to parental illness and death, the reader may wish to refer to Chapter III, Death in the Family.

Before leaving the area of chronic parental illness, however, some guidelines for advising families in the midst of a mother's terminal illness will be given, followed by a case report regarding a child's reactions to his father's *mental* illness.

When a Mother is Fatally Ill

With fortunate and increasing rarity, the need still occasionally arises in any medical practice and in the smallest communities to begin a program of preventive work of an especially difficult sort: preparation of a family for death of their mother. The Center for Preventive Psychiatry has treated one such family for several years and several fatally ill women who have been in treatment for themselves and have provided information concerning their children. A report of these cases is planned at another time. General principles of family management when a mother is dying include the following:

1. Supportive emotional relationship with several family members must be reliably available several days a week for the children and parents.
2. The mother should have as much psychological support as she needs to enable her to discuss with her physician the medical facts of her life, including the probabilities of life-expectancy, so that she can rationally plan for her children's future well-being.
3. The mother's physical burdens should be eased at every acceptable opportunity (unless the mother feels a psychological need to do as much as possible) to enable her maternal capacities to be sustained.
4. Dependency ties which bind children to their mother should be loosened through frequent visits away from the house for preschool children, gradually extending to overnights for latency children; day camps for preschoolers in summer and nursery school in winter; sleep-away summer experiences for at least two weeks for young school children and at least a month for early adolescents; encouragement of out-of-the-house social activities for after school hours and weekends.
5. The children should discuss with the family physician or other expert any questions they have about the mother's condition and prospects.
6. The children should discuss with the mother herself, if she is able, and with the father, their worries and understandings of personal and medical changes.
7. A reliable mother-substitute should come into the home during the terminal phase, preferably a substitute who is willing to stay indefinitely after the death. A wage-earning housekeeper may be adequate, but more ideally another relative should come who is already a fixture in the children's emotional lives.

8. Under no circumstances should the physician or therapist expect that a family is fully capable of carrying out each aspect of the above general program, lest there be an excitation of guilty or anxious feelings in the parents. One case of a woman with far-advanced breast carcinoma, metastatic to her spine and skull as well as to her lungs is relevant to this point. The patient was capable of discussing the realities of her condition and the prognosis with the therapist and a sixteen-year-old daughter. But when the husband learned of these discussions, which she had begun with the daughter before psychotherapy had been arranged, he ultimately forced his wife to withdraw from treatment because of his anger at the therapist for "confronting his wife with what she must forget." In that case there were some conflicts in the husband over his own capacity to bear the physical deterioration already evident in his wife, who had suffered a bilateral mastectomy and consequent distortion of previous sexual relations.

Mental Illness in the Family

CASE REPORT: AN EIGHT-YEAR-OLD BOY WITH A MANIC-DEPRESSIVE FATHER

The following treatment conducted by Myron Harris, Ph.D., was given in the midst of a father's mental illness and was comprised of sixteen sessions in eight months. An ordinarily very conscientious boy, Ned (eight years old), was brought to The Center for Preventive Psychiatry because his mother noticed that he was bringing home "C" grades rather than his usual "A" average. At times he would complain of stomachaches and had "fits of crying." He seemed very fond of his baby brother and not only exhibited great maturity with the infant but also would say (in a hypermature way) that it was important not to disturb or irritate his father. His father had been hospitalized two years previously with manic-depressive illness, and had been at home for the past year. A man with very high standards and cyclical outbreaks of tense dissatisfactions with everyone in the family (including himself), Ned's father was in the midst of plans to move out of the household. He had refused all urgings to return to psychiatric treatment.

The first session. Ned indicated that he thought the therapist might help him with his problem of having to go to religious school, a task which the child disliked. In addition, he apparently hoped that he might gain permission to see the film "Goldfinger," and in fact gained some knowledge from the therapist about a James Bond automobile model which was in the treatment room. The car was used to express a fantasy of "throw the bad guy out," which was also an important theme in his psychological tests—taken a month earlier. In the midst of the session, Ned received an orientation from the therapist about the purpose of their work together, and thus it may be that the emergence of the "throw the bad guy out" was a response by the patient to indicate the importance of his occupation with the father's imminent departure.

The second session. The hint that father occupied Ned's mind was underscored by his depiction of the Irish parliament building. He carefully outlined a drawing of the building, then filled it in with colors and described his father's Irish origin. Next, with unembarrassed expression of ambition, Ned told the therapist of his hope to become Prime Minister of Ireland. A climate of spontaneous communicative freedom had apparently developed quickly, and the child was beginning to trust the therapist with derivatives of his current oedipal strivings and messages about the current reality-stimulated oedipal conflicts. In another moment the "ejector" seated James Bond car was his focus once more, followed by bursts of dart throwing and imaginary rifle shooting. The adult male target of his murderous shooting was suddenly revealed, as the instrument became a machine gun which was aimed at the therapist (drawn on a dart board). At this point no interpretation was made of his ambitions in regard to getting rid of the father and becoming head of his household. There was some hope that simply allowing the derivative fantasies to be expressed and accepted in the therapeutic relationship with an adult male might help "detoxify" their effect. A preliminary formulation was that the child's oedipal strivings were now subject to pathologic inhibition, with resultant intellectual inhibitions, due to the reality of the imminent ejection of the father from the home. But, in addition, a powerful depressing influence was at work because the boy truly loved his father and was in danger of renewed deprivation of his father's companionship.

The third session. Ned described a dream in which Robin took a knife and stabbed him in the heart. Associations included the fact that the boy was a regular reader of the obituary pages and had recently read of a nine-year-old girl who was run over by a car and killed.

In response to the therapist's observation that a boy might be scared of dying or getting killed himself, the patient readily agreed. In an easy flowing way, Ned proceeded to mention that his father had been in the hospital for months because of "sickness." It seemed clearly an idea linked with death. Two themes then emerged quickly and in an intertwined fashion: loneliness and fear. Ned described how children were not allowed to visit in the hospital, but first said that his father would "get very mad" and say things which the patient felt reluctant to repeat. Then, he took courage and quoted some anal-aggressive threats, including, "Stick all that junk up your ass." It was observed to the patient that it must be frightening for him to hear his father get so "mad." This early therapeutic maneuver was aimed at displaying respect for the defensive task and the anxiety involved in the experience.

During the same session, immediately following this display of respect, Ned was able to indicate the similarity of his own impulses and his father's though with some maintenance of distinctions. Telling that he gets mad, too, and says things which are angry, the boy described how he becomes "mad" at his religious school teacher. Later, in the privacy of his own room, he would say, "Go lay a fart, Mrs. . . .!" At this point, the therapist wondered "since all these thoughts are hooked together," whether Ned might be thinking that he might get sick the way his father did, since Ned gets mad, too. Ned then denied that interpretation, and defined his father's trouble as "a sickness." This led to a discussion of his father's medication, and again a return to the theme of loneliness, with an optimistic note from Ned as to how next year he will not be lonely because his brother will be sleeping with him in the same room. He detailed some plans to drill a hole in the wall between his brother's bedroom and his own, and thus appeared to be returning to the penetration aspects of the Robin dream in which a boy stabs another boy. None of the penetration wishes were interpreted. The therapist was content with the patient's having expressed so much so soon about his loneliness and fear. These affects were in clear connection with his father's illness and absence, together with nearly overt indications of concern about identification with the yearned-for man.

The fourth session. Penetration activities again emerged in the form of drilling holes in a model boat, a construction activity to which Ned had looked forward for an entire week since last seeing the therapist. He expressed apprehension about his own body— about not being good at dealing with losing teeth—and dissatisfaction with various weapons, including a water pistol. Toward the end of the hour, he seemed freer and very ambitious: "I'm going to put on the biggest drill and drill through the wood for the rest of the hour." Again, the phallic-level strivings were mixed with separation concerns. He questioned the therapist about how often he would be able to keep coming.

The fifth session. Ned described two old nightmares, expressing surprise that he hadn't already told the therapist one of them: "Haven't I told you about the fox coming through the fire?" In another dream he had thought he was dead and kept screaming in fear after waking up. In still another old dream, there were bad men, especially a certain clown, and many smaller bad men with the clown. "If they were girls I wouldn't be scared, because I could just hit them and chase them away. The men are scary." In this connection Ned described an old fear of prowlers, and it was tentatively observed that Ned seemed to be "scared of something about men, scared that bad men might do something to him." There was no overt response to this interpretation, which was intended to *lead* into an understanding of the boy's confllict between his wish for masculine closeness and his defense against consequences of masculine penetration.

Ned's mother, who attended monthly conferences with the therapist, described that Ned had seemed less comfortable when leaving the sessions the last few times. He had also seemed more withdrawn and occupied with his mother. He was asking questions about her romantic history —when she and his father had first met, how they fell in love, and whether she still loved his father. When Ned's mother gave a friendly kiss to a man who came with his wife to visit, Ned wondered if she loved that man. She described how Ned's father and she had become more and more emotionally detached, but were still living together—although without physical intimacy. Ned's mother had by now started psychiatric treatment of her own, although her husband was still unable to do so.

The sixth session. Ned displayed considerable disgruntlement with his own abilities, complaining that he did not know how to use several instruments in the office, generally wanting a lot of help. He then told of a fantastic "homework machine" which is his prize imaginary possession: "It's twenty acres big. It's in Belfast. (the only place he could find a twenty acre plot that would hold it). It's underground. We got bulldozers and dug a big hole so we could put it there. There's a park, and a path away from it—a secret path."

Ned had found a lot of pieces and put them together. Then, by pressing the button, he found that the machine was doing his homework for him. A lot of men had helped him build this machine, and he gave them one hundred dollars each for their help. It was play money, which the men could give their own children. Ned sends the homework which is on a sheet of paper, by sound waves. The machine in Ireland works on the problem and somehow sends it back with his homework done. There are four guards, still those original helper-men, who protect the place so no one can use it if they discover what it is for.

No interpretation was made regarding this elaborate daydream, which apparently expressed Ned's passive wishes to be helped and cared for by men, relieved of his academic responsibilities. As the fantasy kept coming forth, it took on a more phallic aspect, at least in shape: "[No longer entirely underground] two miles up there is a door. There is a chute going down that door that you get in by. . . . There's an invisible ladder and they go up there like in Batman when they throw the rope up and climb up."

After this expression of hopeful closeness with collaborating males, Ned seemed to shift the theme from his old dread of bad men to a dread of female opposition to his strivings. He had gotten some paint on his shirt, and became anxious about it. Leaving the session, he exclaimed, "I hope my mother doesn't murder me!"

The seventh session. This session was a quiescent one. An interview with Ned's mother revealed that Ned was now more physically adroit, overcoming a prior timidity. He was learning to ride a bicycle, going out on his own with other children. His father was becoming less tense and more at ease with the children. Ned would sometimes garden with him. Ned was making efforts to pull the parents together. He and a seven-year-old girl friend played a game of being host and hostess at a pretend party. They invited Ned's mother and father to come as guests to their "home."

The eighth session. Ned told of a belief that this would be a good time to bring his father into Ned's treatment because his father "is nice now . . . doesn't get mad so much. When he gets mad, that's when he went to the hospital." At this point, Ned began shooting darts at a picture of the therapist, threatening to hit him in the eye, disappointed because he couldn't succeed. He laughed and denied there were any feeling of being angry about the proposed talk with his father. But a fantasy emerged about "bad friends" who outnumbered him. This led to telling about recent experiences with an enemy who pulled out plants from Ned's family garden. He told his father, who was also angry, "If you see someone with a fat eye, bloody lips and teeth hanging out, you'll know I did it." "I was even madder than my father was." Ned added that usually he wins when he fights because he uses all of his power—which is a secret his enemies don't know about him. Occupied with a model, he emphasized his pleasure in getting the masts up. "That's the best part of it." Perhaps the darts were phallic-aggressive in their significance, as was his final communication in the session in which he bounced silly putty all around the room—demonstrating his ability to leave the therapist helpless about the timing of the termination, which he successfully delayed.

In this session, Ned's fantasies of penetration and phallic power were more of an active variety, the power being his own and he being the penetrator. Rather than fearing bad men or his father, he overcame the bad men and was his father's ally. The therapist seemed to be the target of his aggressions here (the target of the penetrating darts), while the father is exempt. Ned was now able to share realistic assessments of his father with the therapist, commenting in a rather neutral way about the fluctuations in his father's mood while forcefully bringing the therapist's attention to Ned's own violent impulses ("even madder than my father. . . .") *This focus away from the external onto the internal is probably a valuable shift, desirable in any emergency psychotherapy with a relatively intact child.*

An interview with Ned's father. Expressing concern that he and Ned had not been close, the father wished that Ned would confide in him more. He seemed to be taking more pleasure in his son's company, and was enjoying making plans about baseball games. The man did not regard himself as a good model for Ned, especially because of his tendency to perfectionism and social withdrawal. The therapist focussed on the problem that the father worried so much about Ned becoming like him that this handicapped the development of a freer relationship between himself and his son—especially because he constantly pushed Ned to do better and better. The father expressed some understanding that he was treating Ned in some ways as if Ned were himself—with the same attitude of driving for higher achievement in work (school). To the therapist's surprise, the father accepted a recommendation that he return to psychiatric treatment. Possibly the work done with his son had led to a favorable climate for accepting the recommendation as a humane one rather than as harshly critical.

The ninth session. Assiduous work on the model was combined with hope that the interview with the father might lead to the father getting Ned a present!

The tenth session. Ned was no longer reading obituary pages. Now he was reading about how people get arrested for traffic violations. The therapist wondered if, since Ned used to read obituary pages when he was afraid of dying, now he was reading about people getting tickets because he was afraid of getting tickets or somehow breaking the law. Ned stated that sometimes he goes riding through a stop signal on his bicycle, or rides on the wrong side of the street.

Soon Ned would be going away to day camp, and already was looking forward to sleep-away camp the next summer. He then discussed a worry he had about a female counselor, to whom his group had been assigned. He rolled his eyes apprehensively, and the therapist asked if this was connected with having to dress and undress in front of her. "Yeah, but if she was a teenager I wouldn't get undressed at all. But she's almost out of the university, so she's more like a . . . ." Here the therapist had to supply the word "mother." Ned pointed to his own genital area, and said that teenage girls wouldn't know about "that junk," giggling. He expressed the thought that people keep from talking about these parts of the body because they keep it hidden. However, he and another group of children, including a girl two years younger, had played a game using "bathroom" words.

Apparently Ned was now feeling frightened about his own daring, and, having lost some inhibitions (bicycle, use of forbidden words), he was distressed by what might happen next. Perhaps he would commit the oedipal crime of undressing in front of a—he cannot say it—mother! The ease with which these matters came to therapeutic attention suggests a good prognosis, and the interviews with his parents, lately with his father, seemed to facilitate Ned's trust in the therapist as well as his ease in coping with his "forbidden" impulses.

The eleventh session. Resistant to efforts to draw him out, Ned threw a dart which missed the board and penetrated a large ball—deflating it.

An interview with Ned's father. The desirablility of treatment for the father was once more discussed, so far nothing having come of his intention to resume. He was concerned because Ned seemed to have all parental function from his mother. Even sexual education was being done by the mother, and Ned was not asking his father anything about the process of reproduction.

The twelfth session. Ned's effort to use a baseball and bat inside the playroom led to the therapist being frightened that he would be hit when Ned used the bat. Ned noticed the fear, commented on it, and the therapist confirmed the perception. A more acceptable activity was planned, the problem discussed freely. Ned decided to put another sail on his boat model. There would be a two-month vacation after the next session, but the therapist was not yet dealing with the impending separation. Ned probably was dealing with a highly disguised derivative of the separation problem by trying to experiment with getting rid of the therapist in a dangerous game, turning the passively experienced separation into one created by Ned himself.

The thirteenth session. Ned announced his awareness of the impending departure by declaring, "I think I'll call the boat finished," sitting down and smiling. At that point the therapist apologized for not having realized in the last session that there would only be one more meeting time before vacation. The two made plans for meeting after the summer, but Ned's response was to demonstrate great independence. In response to offers of practical assistance in mounting and blowing up balloons which he was using as dart targets, Ned responded: "*I* can do it." He tried hard to show how hard he could pitch a baseball, and became mischievous and more daring than ever with a squirt gun. Another child had written,

"The doctor is a big fat fink" upon the dart board, and Ned wrote, "Yes," under it. This daring and provocative behavior was observed to the patient with the statement that Ned must be feeling some satisfaction in being able to do more daring and adventurous things lately, and that perhaps there was also a connection to feelings about going away from the doctor. Ned seemed to be expressing himself in action—a kind of aggressive experimentation with his relationship to his therapist. At the end of the session, there was more expression through action, smiling, lingering, friendly, and taking his own boat home.

The next four sessions with Ned occurred after his summer vacation. Essentially they were concerned with his reactions to the separation and to the impending termination. These two experiences gave him an opportunity to work through, while still in treatment, some of his angry feelings about being abandoned by his father.

The fourteenth session. Ned played a game of "Shoot Mike Harris," using the therapist's first name. He showed the doctor how he learned to throw a football. Within a short time he went through a quick series of demonstrations—showing skill in throwing a baseball, kicking a ball, and shooting a gun. He began to shoot directly at the doctor with a pop-gun, and made balloons explode directly in the doctors ears. His anger was observed to him and interpreted as being not just anger: "I think you are glad to see me. . . . Isn't it funny, you're really glad to see me, glad to be back here, but you keep shooting me and throwing things at me; and I guess maybe that's the way you say hello."

Explicit discussion was initiated in this session regarding the planned number of sessions remaining. Ned looked shocked when told that there were three more sessions expected. He took an active position: "Then you can come to visit me." He grew very quiet, the therapist remarked that he knew Ned didn't like the idea of stopping, and that Ned would like to keep coming. The child confirmed this interpretation by looking around and making plans to build an extremely complicated model. This action was translated by observing that perhaps Ned figured he could keep on working here for a long time with that model. Smiling, Ned looked down in a gesture of agreement. He then ended the session with mixtures of sad soberness, compliance and defiance. Saying, "Now I'll clean up the table," he pushed little pieces of a model onto the floor where they would have to be picked up again. He was quiet and sober when going out of the office to meet his mother in the waiting room.

The fifteenth session. Early in the hour Ned announced his concern about the impending separation. He failed to ring the bell, so that he made himself be kept waiting longer than necessary. He started saying "ugly fink," "stupid," and other aggressive appellations which seemed to have no bearing on his feelings toward the therapist except in regard to losing him. These remarks were interpreted as letting the doctor know how Ned felt about the next session being the last time they would see each other—for a few months, at least. Ned picked up some darts and threw them hard at the dart board and threateningly at the clown. Therapist: "I guess this is another way of letting me know how bad this makes you feel." Ned took a water pistol, showed it to the doctor, and ran to fill it with water. Coming back, he started shooting at the therapist, who had to defend himself with a towel. Then Ned pulled out the plug and dripped water over the playroom floor, saying, "I'm peeing all over the playroom floor. You have to wipe it all up!" Therapist: "Having to be without me makes you feel like breaking all the rules and peeing on my floor."

After having expressed this burst of resentment which was accepted by the therapist as an important communication about how hard it was to be without him, Ned was able to be more overtly friendly. He came close to sitting on the doctor's lap, making light kissing sounds as his face almost touched the doctor's. When this behavior became very clearly established, the therapist said, "How tough it is when you like someone very much and want to show it, like thinking of kissing me like you kiss your Daddy, while at the same time you feel hurt and mad because it sounds like I don't want to be seeing you regularly any more." Ned made a brief assay at indifference: "Who cares?" Then he went on working with the therapist on the model, occasionally adopting a threatening tone.

Ned assured himself that if he didn't finish the model he could take it home with him at the end of the next (last regularly-scheduled) session. This was agreed upon. The patient was tacitly encouraged in his feeling that he was able to get satisfaction without direct help of the therapist.

The sixteenth session. Although coming in with stormy aggressive play, and even puncturing a plastic chair with a dart, Ned melted into forthright dealing with the separation problem when the therapist forbade him to damage the furniture and discussed with him the importance of setting a followup appointment time. Ned seemed pleased and surprised to have the matter considered so seriously, and rather gently asked if the therapist could come to visit at his home for Thanksgiving. Accepting the frustration of this friendly wish, Ned created an intimacy, nevertheless, by calling the therapist by his first name—as if this were the natural way to call him. At the end of the session, when some glue was lacking for completion of the model, Ned said, "That's all right, we can buy some." Thus he ended on a note of comraderie and self-sufficiency, but also with clear recognition of the value of his therapy. To underline his feelings about the need to be seen again, Ned made his parting topic an insistence that the doctor make sure to speak to his mother about making the followup appointment. He had thus taken over the doctor's role to a valuable and constructive extent, containing within the identification an activity which ensured the continuation of his relationship.

Followup—(five weeks later)—the seventeenth session. Ned smiled a big smile and asked if there were any new models, spotting one on which he would like to work. Aggressive behavior began by blowing up balloons and popping them very close to the therapist, progressing to shaking his fist when dissatisfied with the therapist's work on the model. Then he sat down. Asked if he remembered when he used to come in and call names and throw things around, Ned confirmed that he remembered. He added that he also used to squirt water from the pistol at the therapist. When these actions were related to Ned's feeling disappointed about not coming regularly, Ned confirmed the interpretation by being verbally and physically abusive, and then requesting that his mother bring him back within the next month.

At the end of eight months, Ned had progressed well clinically. His treatment had allowed some clear communications to emerge concerning his own angry feelings and his dreads that his angry feelings might be related to his father's "mad" and sick behavior. His loneliness for masculine relationships had apparently led to distorted expressions in the form of fears that "bad men" would attack him. During treatment a more accepting attitude developed toward his own yearnings, allowing a lively and forthright set of love expressions to emerge, directed at the male therapist. Several interpretations of the defense against these feelings were made, particularly in regard to anger emerging when his love for the therapist had to be frustrated by separation. It is hoped that Ned has been strengthened in dealing with his love for his father, via being strengthened in dealing with love for the therapist.

CHAPTER III

Death in the Family

IN RECENT YEARS medical advances have raised some doubts as to whether death is as certain as taxes. Heart-attack victims, actually legally dead because of the cessation of heart beats, can be "restored" to life by half a dozen means. Yet these semantic quibblings about what constitutes the moment of death do little to change the psychological fact that death of a loved person—by whatever timing—is a hazard to the survivor's mental health.

Three lines of evidence point to the importance to public health of psychiatric problems following death in the family. The foremost and best-developed line of evidence is a large series of *retrospective* studies. These show highly significant correlations between childhood bereavement and later-life emotional illness, as well as between loss of a spouse and adult emotional illness. The two other lines of evidence are *anterospective* (prospective or future-looking) studies of the consequences of bereavement, and *clinical case studies* of psychiatric patients who happen to have been bereaved. An orientation to all three lines of evidence will be given in this chapter because the psychiatric problems involved seem so pressing and the opportunities for prevention seem ripe.

Retrospective Studies of Adult Mental Illness and History of Childhood Bereavement

An exquisite study, convincingly showing correlations between the incidence of childhood bereavement and the degree of adult depression was performed by Beck and Seth in Philadelphia (1963). A group of 297 inpatients and outpatients was studied. Their degree of depression was investigated with use of a depression inventory and clinical ratings by experienced psychiatrists. One hundred "very depressed" patients showed a significantly higher incidence of orphanhood before age sixteen (27 per cent) than did the hundred "least depressed" patients (12 per cent). There was also a tendency for the very depressed group to have had more early-life parental death—before age four—than the least depressed group.

Similar findings, not so well controlled for degrees of depression, were reported earlier by Brown (1961). Still less systematic, but impressive and pioneering studies by Hilgard and Newman (1960) and Barry and Lindemann (1960) all point to a general association between early childhood bereavement and later adult hospitalization for psychiatric illness. These latter studies failed to take into account some important demographic variables. No study has been reported which considers all relevant demographic variables and at the same time the psychiatric diagnosis, age of *onset* of psychiatric illness, age of patient at time of parental death, sex of patient, and sex of parent who died.

It seems likely that childhood experience of bereavement can only contribute to, rather than cause, a psychiatric illness. Therefore the influence of childhood bereavement, so clearly known to analysts and families who observe its noxious effects, can best be observed on a statistical basis by taking into account not only the incidence of psychiatric illness in a bereaved population, but also the questions of early onset, intensity, and type of illness. Lacking such global approaches, a clear appreciation of the pathogenic force of childhood bereavement has not yet been attained.

Sociopathy and Homes Broken by Death or Divorce

There is a strong correlation between parental loss (for any reason) in childhood and later development of sociopathy. The Gluecks' classic retrospective study (1950) was the first to show indisputably a massive correlation in a carefully controlled manner. Greer's more recent retrospective study from Australia (1964) also contains a suitable control system. Like the Gluecks, Greer found that 60 per cent of sociopaths seen in an outpatient clinic suffered the absence or death of a parent in childhood. The minimum period of absence considered was twelve months. The control figures were less than 30 per cent for both neurotic patients and the control subjects. (Total: 387 neurotics, 79 sociopaths, 691 controls.)

As with adult depressed patients, there is a tendency for sociopaths to have early-life parental loss. Of those who experienced childhood parental loss, sociopaths differed significantly from the neurotic patients in the age at which the loss was experienced. Seventy per cent of the sociopaths with a history of parent loss had been subject to that presumably pathogenic experience before age five.

Only 36 per cent of neurotics with parent loss had that experience before age five. (Unfortunately control figures for the general population are not given in this aspect.)

Greer also found that loss of *both* parents was distinctly more common among sociopaths than neurotics. Fifteen of the 47 sociopaths with history of loss had lost both parents. This compared with 15 out of 110 neurotics.

As in studies by Barry and Lindemann, Greer reported a correlation between sex and the impact of parent loss. A greater proportion of Greer's female sociopaths suffered parental loss than the male sociopaths. The same was true for Greer's neurotics (Table 1).

TABLE 1—*Per cent with parental loss for at least one year by age fifteen*

	Control	Neurotic	Sociopath
Male	29	24	51
Female	25	31	77

ANTEROSPECTIVE FINDINGS AFTER CHILDHOOD BEREAVEMENT

Other than the study reported by the author later in this chapter (p. 74), the only anterospective data of an organized sort is that collected by Gregory (1965). Gregory scrutinized various social, adademic and biographical factors in a statewide sample of 11,329 Minnesota ninth-graders from 86 different communities. There was a good representation of diverse economic and geographic areas, and the sample included 28 per cent of the entire ninth-grade population in the state. Data relevant to this chapter included information on orphanhood, parental divorce or separation, remarriage, and data on parental social and economic status.

Three years after the original sampling, a student-by-student followup was made regarding high-school dropouts and juvenile delinquency. A rating of degree of delinquency was made for each child, from zero to four. Four indicated a pattern of repeated serious offences.

The highest rates of delinquency were found among boys whose parents were separated or divorced and among those who were living with the mother only. Higher than average delinquency rates were also found among boys who had lost a father by death. Rates of delinquency among boys living with their father only were quite near to average, whether the boys had lost a mother by death, separation or divorce. This corroborates the Gluecks' finding that paternal absence is more critical than maternal absence in the development of juvenile delinquency in boys.

Among girls, the highest rates of delinquency were found in separated or divorced families, most impressively in families where the girls live with fathers only. Loss of a mother by death was associated with a higher rate of delinquency than loss of a father by death. As with boys, the same-sex bereavement disposes to delinquency more than opposite-sex bereavement.

The above data were controlled for social and economic status, and also for intelligence levels. Similar controls were necessary regarding the question of highschool dropouts. Since this symptom is closely related to juvenile delinquency, an effort to separate the data concerning dropouts and delinquency was made. Even among *nondelinquent* boys and girls, high rates of dropout were found among those who had been bereaved of the same-sex parent. Marital separation and divorce had similar associations with high rates of school dropouts (see Table 2).

TABLE 2 (from Gregory, 1965)

	Delinquency Rates (Severe Delinquency)		School Dropouts	
	Boys (per cent)	Girls (per cent)	Boys (per cent)	Girls (per cent)
Family intact	23	10	14	10
Father dead	29	10	25	18
Mother dead	26	18	19	21
Both dead	30	13	29	29
Separated or divorced	37	21	27	26
Father dead, child living with with mother only	50	(no data comparably tabulated)		
Mother dead, child living with father only	40	(no data comparably tabulated)		
Living with father only	26	21	21	27
Living with mother only	35	15	27	21

Clinical Studies

This area contains a vast literature, although not always rich in observation. A selective sampling rather than comprehensive review will be attempted at this point.

Maternal Death During Infancy

Rene Spitz (1951) considers that all disease-producing psychological influences during infancy are unsatisfactory mother-child relations—either the wrong kind of relations or insufficient amounts. The wrong kind is called "psychotoxic," including severe rejection of the child, anxious overpermissiveness, and hostilities disguished as anxieties. Insufficient or emotionally deficient mother-child relationships include partial and total deprivation of relationship to the mother or mother-substitute. In cases of total maternal deprivation, particularly where the mother-child relationship has gone on for at least a few months, total cessation of such relationship leads to a wide variety of profound mental and physical damage. Such children at the end of an additional year's time sometimes achieve only 50 per cent of the normal expected developmental level. Often they do not sit, stand or talk until age four. Bizarre finger movements and spasmus nutans are observed in some. Many of these children die of physical diseases and nonspecific wasting. Thirty-four out of 91 children followed by Spitz for two years died.

Provence and Lipton (1962) have documented the effects of institutional environment on 75 infants. Deprivation of a constant maternal influence was one factor which led to marked developmental retardation. Deficiencies or retardations were apparent in motor development, impulse control, verbal abilities, and social relationships. In addition to retardation in those areas, there was also conspicuous disuse of available functions.

Some General Aspects of Early Childhood Separations and Bereavement

Bowlby, Spitz, Provence, Lipton and others have been primarily concerned with absence of a mother in the preoedipal phases of life. However, this review will highlight more of the oedipal-phase reactions, considering the earlier area only to touch upon Anna Freud's work because it is applicable when studying the reactions of older children.

Taking a broad view of the immediate pathological effects of separation, including death of a parent, Miss Freud (1960) lists four sets of difficulties:

1. Psychosomatic problems ranging from sleeping, feeding and digestive disturbances to increased susceptibility to upper respiratory infections.

2. Instinctual regressions in both libidinal and aggressive expressions, and at worst a "diffusion of libidinal and aggressive elements which allow the latter to dominate."

3. Regressions of ego-functions, usually the functions most endangered being those which have most recently been acquired. Very impressive to Miss Freud were loss of speech, bowel and bladder control, and decline of social adaptations.

4. Disturbances of libido distribution. During the process of withdrawal of libido from the mental representative of the mother, hypochondriacal disturbances result from the use of the newly available libido to cathect the child's own body. When the self-image is increasingly cathected, a variety of problems may result, including omnipotent ideas. If the child already has a crude inner fantasy world, this may become overcathected with a resultant autism. If separation from the mother is permanent, as in the death of the mother, the pathologic development may become irreversible.

Miss Freud stresses that, considered from all points of view, the state of the child's psychological development at the time of the loss is crucial in determining whether pathologic consequences will ensue. Particularly decisive is "whether at the moment of losing the mother the tie to her is primarily narcissistic or whether personal and affectionate elements had begun to predominate, transforming the attachment into object love . . . ." If love with "object-constancy" had been attained, then the painful "disengagement process known to us as mourning" will be necessary before libido can be removed from the mental representative of the lost object. Upon bereavement, some of the child's ego-functions may be overwhelmed by the problem of dealing with the painful affect of grief, or he may develop pathologic solutions of oedipal problems. With the advent of strong object-constancy, usually the child is already grappling with later developmental problems, including those of guilty reactions.

Sigmund Freud, in *Mourning and Melancholia* (1917), noted that the loss of a loved person is pathogenic in proportion to the pre-existing degree of ambivalence toward that person. Severe pre-existing guilt feelings lead to a pathogenic outcome, often ending in suicide. He did not comment in that work on the special experience of childhood death of a parent, but earlier (1900) reported on the reality-testing problem of a 10-year-old paternally-bereaved boy who complained, "I know father's dead, but what I can't understand is why he doesn't come home for supper." He also noted (1910, 1915) the homosexual disposition of children living with the same-sex parent.

Helene Deutch (1937) describes cases in which loss of a parent is associated with absence of affective response whether in childhood or adult life. Other economic changes then occur: massive defenses with absence of affect throughout all phases of object relations; displacement of affect in a shallow fashion to other areas of object relations; or increased narcissistic investment of libido. She presents four illustrative cases. Deutsch conceives of parental death in childhood as being frequently pathogenic not only because of the child's intellectual inability to comprehend the finality of death, or weak development of object libido. It is also, and perhaps more frequently, pathogenic because of the immature ego's inability to bear the prolonged painful affects of grief. Deutsch postulates an undescribed mechanism by which, when a parent dies, the ego recognizes an overwhelming quantity of affect is about to be released. Next, a primitive mechanism of defense is postulated which, having been set in motion by the previous recognition and a signal, begins massive defense against the emergence of the painful affects. Furthermore, object cathexis is transformed into narcissistic cathexis. Still further, the defensive work transforms some mental events from a secondary-process state into a primary-process state so that there is a highly displaceable quality to the cathexes which have been withdrawn from the object representative. Affects formerly associated with the object representatives are liable to reappear inappropriately. There is chronic pressure for discharge of the defended-against affects, which often reappear as "unmotivated depressions," sometimes lasting for a lifetime.

Deutsch's thinking about unmotivated depressions as a consequence of absent-affect following parental death is supported by Beck's previously cited study of depressed and nondepressed patients (1963) showing that childhood bereavement is significantly more frequent in the depressed group. In Beck's profoundly depressed group the age of parental death is significantly earlier than in the mildly depressed group. Presumably the youngest age groups are least able to express the defended-against affects.

Loretta Bender (1954), in a seldom-noted contribution to literature on childhood bereavement, describes a series of eleven children who poignantly illustrate Deutsch's point that "the ego is rent asunder in those children who do not employ the usual defenses, and who mourn as an adult does." Deutsch notes that quantitative factors as well as qualitative development factors may determine whether and to what extent damage occurs. "If the intensity of the affects is too great, or if the ego is relatively weak, the aid of defensive and rejecting mechanisms is invoked." If an adult's ego-strength happens to be diverted at the time of parental death—for example, by exhaustion or because of some immediately preceding painful occurrence, "the residual energy is unable to cope with the exigent demands of mourning." In a child, the ego is usually weak for developmental reasons and a pathologic outcome, therefore, is more likely to be inevitable.

Deutsch's writing on this subject, although brief, is packed with observations and formulations important for preventive work. She believes it is essential to later emotional health that *every real loss of a loved person must be reacted to with a complete process of mourning so that no "early libidinal or aggressive attachments persist."* Whenever any form of affect exclusion appears, for whatever reason, "the quantity of the painful reaction intended for the neglected direct mourning must be mastered."

Ernst Kris (1956) reports the case of a young female psychologist whose mother died when the patient was three years old. Kris noted a "libidinization of the function of reminiscing itself." Investment of libido in the function of memories seems to be a result of desiring "to be close to those she had loved early in life." In addition, "talk of the past served to counter-balance the drab present." Further, while the tensions of the present were threatening, she was master of those she conjured in recollection." Kris notes that "a repressed unconscious fantasy can be treated like a possession or a loved object."

Specific Oedipal Problems Following Parental Loss

Leonardo da Vinci suffered the absence of a father until age four. Being the only solace of his mother, he was open to her "tender seductions" (Freud, 1910). Freud attributed da Vinci's later homosexuality partly to the mother's reciprocated libidinal tie to him, in lieu of her husband. Five years later (in *Three Essays on the Theory of Sexuality*), Freud stated "the early loss of one of their parents by death, divorce or separation . . . [produces the] result that the remaining parent absorbs the whole of the child's love, determines the sex of the person who is later to be chosen as a sexual object and may thus open the way to permanent inversion."

Ferenczi (1914) noted that loss of a father and the resultant lack of "unavoidable conflicts between father and son" dispose to male homosexuality. Fenichel (1931) emphasized the guilt which results from fulfillment of oedipal wishes through death of the same-sex parent and the danger of idealization when the opposite-sex parent dies.

Anna Freud (1943, 1944) observed fatherless children at the Hampstead Nurseries during World War II. These children were strongly involved with a fantasied father even when no father had been known to them at all. Superego development proceeded to some extent with the fantasied father. Nunberg (1932) inferred that fatherless children often behave as if they have no guilt feelings—ruthlessly, as if revenging themselves on a world which has failed to provide a father.

Margaret Meiss (1952) described the analysis of a five-year-old boy (Peter) whose father had died when the child was age three years, three months. At the time of entering analysis, Peter showed evidence of being in the phallic phase and having considerable difficulty resolving oedipal problems. He suffered from insomnia and fear that his mother would die. He heard voices inside his head which said, "Daddy is angry," and told "about times I didn't like Daddy, times when Daddy was angry at me."

It was Meiss's purpose to point out the specific effects of paternal bereavement as it influenced a child who would have become neurotic in any event. Features of the neurosis which could be attributed, at least in part, to the specific experience are the special focus of her essay. Meiss believes the child's anxiety about his mother dying probably would not have appeared without the father's death. He had a fantasy that through the mother's death the parents would be reunited forever, and he would be entirely alone. Unlike usual fears of a parent's death, this symptom was not largely the result of antagonism toward the mother but stemmed more from the child's oedipal rivalry with the dead father.

Another special feature of Peter's analysis was the quality of his transference. He was sexually excited during his analytic hours, though calm and detached at home. Meiss believes that "the death of the father . . . promoted a precocious internationalization of his [father's] prohibitions. . . . There was no actual father present to reassure the child that wishes are not the same as deeds, or to continue giving and evoking affection; his fearsome image could not be tested against reality." This excessively harsh fantasied father figure and its contribution to the superego through an unusually intense identification due to object-loss contributed to superego functioning of a sort which heightened transference reactions. Peter consistently used the analyst's husband as a "substitute for a father" in the analytic fantasies. Meiss believes that the child's overwhelming fear of his dead father may have made it too dangerous for him to return to his original object (the mother). The analyst was safer because her husband seemed less threatening than his invisible and omniscient parent.

Meiss cites a variety of other factors which went into the formation of this child's neurosis, including multiple separations beginning at age 9 months, a tonsillectomy at 19 months, the loss of a brother through institutionalization at 20 months, and the death of a newborn brother when the patient was 24 months old. Meiss does not comment on the terrible guilts which the two fraternal losses may have engendered prior to the father's death, for which the patient also felt guilty.

His father's death was fused in Peter's mind with memories concerning other people who had left him. The little boy was occupied with thoughts that his daddy was angry at him. However, he attributed to an absent German maid the statement that his penis could be bitten off. He could not be reassured about the impossibility of such a thing happening to him until told that his father, if alive, would explain to him that his penis could not be bitten off. It should be made clear, too, that Peter's oedipal rivalry antedated his father's death considerably. For this reason, the child might well have been troubled by sleeplessness and prowling about at night without bereavement.

The question of what factors led to the outbreak of Peter's symptoms, about age five is interesting since the death occurred 21 months previously. Meiss speculates that physiological increments in Peter's phallic drive exacerbated the latent conflict. Another factor disposing to this particular timing of neurotic outbreak was that the mother had entered therapy, which led to a diminution of her sadistic treatment of the child. As she became more truly affectionate with him, the child must have felt a dangerous gratification of his wish to replace the father in his mother's love life. Again, whether these last two factors would have been so dangerous in the presence of a real father is problematic.

Reviewing the literature from 1930 to 1954, Neubauer (1960) found five female and five male analytic cases with material centered about a one-parent relationship. All but two had lost a parent before the oedipal phase and all ten had only one parent during the oedipal phase. Eisendorfer (1943) analyzed two fatherless women with increased primary homosexual attachment to their mothers. They identified with their absent fathers to keep their mothers' love during their oedipal phases. Annie Reich (1954), in analyzing a paternally bereaved girl, found that desexualization of fantasies about her dead father was not possible. "No stable identification was possible with nonsexual qualities of object that existed in her fantasy only. The normal impact of reality on this fantasy object . . . [left] the unsublimated phallic character of the ego ideal and its megalomanic scope. " . . . [when] sexual characteristics as such remain an ego ideal, a fixation on or regression to primitive, aggressive, pregenital levels is frequent, which leads to a persistence of particularly cruel superego forerunners."

Neubauer's own analysand experienced nearly total absence of her father (1960). Rita, three-and-one-half at the onset of analysis, was one week old when her father left. Her presenting problems included excessive eating and "sexual confusion" with an "expressed wish to be a boy." Her father returned for two visits at the mother's importuning when the child was already in treatment. He added to Rita's burdens at that time by yielding to her pleas that she be allowed to watch him urinate. He also teased her by calling her, "Hey, boy!" tauntingly, undermining her frail sense of conviction as to whether she had ever possessed a penis or was born a girl.

Like Meiss's patient whose opposite-sex parent was absent before phallic development began, Rita became anxious with the onset of that development. She began to long for her father, and in her loneliness wished to be a male herself. While not suffering from separation problems before, she—like Meiss's motherless boy—began reacting with severe anxiety. Castration anxiety was now apparently reinforcing separation anxiety. Rita became unable to attend a day nursery where she was party to other children's sexual play. She pleaded to stay home, complaining she had been a boy the week before but now had lost her penis.

In panic and fury after two weeks of school she attacked her mother, screamed for hours, undressed and urinated on the floor. It was at this point the father made his addition to Rita's burdens. After her father's visit Rita apparently turned even more to him rather than to "regression to a demanding pregenital relationship to mother." However, father implicitly expressed the demand that she be a boy and this she strenuously strove to be in play. Never fully at ease with her own wish for a penis, she retreated at times from related issues. For example, she decided never to get married. Reality-testing was seriously threatened by her overidealization of the again-absent father, whom she thought of as a protective, all-powerful, all-loving person. When he cynically broke a promise to visit her at the therapeutic nursery she was attending, Rita claimed that he had really come but had been refused permission to enter.

Neubauer observes that events may "have an extraordinarily traumatic effect for a child suffering from oedipal deficiency." Lacking the "day-to-day interplay between the child and each parent, . . . synchronization and dosing of oedipal experiences in a continuous reality content," and observations "of the primal scene with all its social equivalents—developmental forces crystallize too suddenly around events rather than being slowly but continuously interwoven in experience."

Shambaugh (1961) made a special contribution, as did Furman (1964) later in describing the reactions of a child to the death of a parent where the child was well-known to the therapist before the death. Some problems of retrospective distortion were thereby avoided. Seven-year-old Henry was seen by Shambaugh for five months, having been brought by his father for preventive work during the mother's terminal months. The dying mother's refusal to allow treatment, and the father's rapid remarriage to an immature woman suggest that there may have been significant pre-existing weakness in the parents' psychological health. Before the mother interrupted treatment, it was observed that Henry started to "suppress" angry feelings toward her which had been excited by her increasingly stern demands for high academic performance.

After a seven-month interruption, Henry resumed treatment shortly after his mother's death. He was then pathologically hyperactive, distractable, gay and even euphoric. Any attempt by the therapist to discuss his mother's death was met with anxiety, anger and avoidance, even by running out of the office. He felt cheated in all games he played in the sessions, and made countless demands for toys and food. Play themes were violent. Object-relationships were profoundly altered. He began to treat his four-year-old sister with parental tenderness and concern, often consoling her. He became clinging toward his father and used baby talk, while simultaneously belittling the man and denying that he needed him. His attachment increased as father found a woman. Then Henry imagined lying in the sun all day with father, or riding on horses with him. He began sharing the father's bed. Simultaneous with this homosexual trend, an anxiety-laden desire for physical closeness to the male therapist developed. Henry then welcomed his new stepmother (married after a four-month courtship) and gave up his homosexual orientation with apparent relief. It was only following this marriage that Henry went through some mourning work. He became sad, serious, recalled his mother's chest surgery and tried to obey her injunction to stop treatment. He began treasuring a few objects she had given him, but also learned to accept his stepmother's taste in refurnishing the home differently from his mother.

Henry's reaction had thus included "regression to orality, anger and fantasies of violence." He withdrew libidinal investment from his remaining objects with an increased narcissism, "to the point of megalomanic fantasies of independence." His efforts to mourn by consciously thinking of his mother and gradually decathecting memories of her foundered because of his childish ego's inability to bear the associated painful affect. Instead he had to regress.

Remus-Araico (1964) writes of twelve adult analysands who were bereaved during childhood. Eight cases were Araico's own patients and four were in analysis with his students. Two women had suffered paternal bereavement, and two had suffered maternal bereavement. Two males had suffered maternal bereavement, and six paternal bereavement. All patients, Araico found, showed high sensitivity to adulthood object losses. Each feared going to a new place. Each displayed what seemed to be an infantile traumatic neurosis with fixation to the infantile stage of mourning. Each patient had been forced into "emergency economic adjustments" with a sudden, accelerated tempo of introjection, leading to a kind of psychological "choking." He noted a tendency for his patients to observe a "cult of the lost object," in which the child begins to preserve the lost relationship secretly. The cult was disguised by borrowing common cultural and religious objects. The deepest tenderness was shown in these private communions, which resembled the creation of a religion. The idealization involved became a defense against the affective discharge features of mourning.

A unique contribution of Araico's study is his deliberate use of "timeless sessions" in four patients. These consisted of up to five extra sessions per patient. The extra sessions were scheduled at hours which enabled the analyst to proceed essentially without any limit to duration except that of mutual fatigue. At times Araico and his co-workers found the catharsis and revivication of memories by this means extremely intense: "We felt as if we were re-experiencing mourning before the corpse." The technique has much to commend it and could be studied to determine whether some phenomena occur which are not obtained in other aspects of the same patient's analysis. It may resemble the effects of hypnotic "revivication" techniques in facilitation of recall and catharsis.

Maternal Death During Childbirth, Delayed Consequences

Among many special forms of parental deprivation, one more will be considered, and that most incompletely. It involves the death of a child's mother during the infant's birth—a circumstance which has not yet been made the subject of organized inquiry. Although harmful consequences might regularly come from a little girl's associations of maternal function with death, no literature can be found on this particular experience with the exception of the little-appreciated contribution of Marie Bonaparte (1939). Bonaparte's autobiographical *Five Copy Books* describe with great documentation the profound dreads of female sexuality she suffered as an apparent consequence of her own mother's death at her own birth. It is of interest that in her theorizing Marie Bonaparte believes "the little girl seems to have an organic intuition that sexuality is a menace to her, to the vital interior of her body. . . . Even in the absence of [frightening] experience, a kind of instinct of self-preservation seems to pre-exist in the female mammal, an instinct which causes her first reaction to be flight from the male pursuit."* The theory appears dictated less by observation of female mammals than by the author's knowledge early in life of her mother's death shortly after childbirth, a fact which was frequently told to her and which colored her early attitudes toward sexual activities. She speaks also of a "biological" fear, namely, the vital fear of penetration of the interior of the living substance. "Women envy the penis because it alone permits the longed for return to the mother's body and because it alone permits a centrifugal sex act. Thus it appears as the counter-offensive weapon best adapted to avert the centripetal threat to the interior of the body."

Bonaparte describes hallucinations of "dyed" creatures which she experienced at age nine, and of which she made notes on the day they actually occurred: "I was writing in my diary and I saw horrible faces, some square and some pointed, and bodies without heads. In short, all the most horrible things that one could imagine coming into the room . . . On another occasion in the same month, in waking up I was on my left side and in turning to the right I saw on the prie-dieu the Chateinier (an imaginary dyed animal); I immediately hid under the blanket with 'closed eyes' and that is how I avoided it." In discussing these hallucinations Bonaparte reports that she also had a previous episode of hallucinations at age four.† She relates that she awoke one morning and spat blood. She then saw a multicolored stork perched on her abdomen. Although Bonaparte does not comment on it, it seems clear that her vision of a stork at the time of spitting blood must have been overdetermined by her own mother having died of tuberculosis in connection with her own birth.

---

* M. Bonaparte, Five Copy Books. London, Imago, 1950, Vol. 2, p. 235.

† *Ibid.*, p. 42.

The spitting of blood reminded her of her own mother's hemoptysis. The stork represented the birth. The hallucination of an imaginary animal (the dyed Chateinier) at age nine has to be understood among all its implications, as including the idea of a cat that has been killed (dyed). The already multi-lingual nine-year-old child unconsciously may have been making a pun on the double-meaning word in relation to death.

Rather than report further on this rich document, the review will rest with Bonaparte's own words, written after her analysis by Freud: ". . . the impression on me which still survives in my unconscious: namely, that all women are more or less dead, or at least candidates for death, while men, the bearers of the phallus, are immortal. Sometimes in certain hypnagogic states, I find myself astonished that there are innumerable women on the face of the earth, and not men only."*

Eighteen Untreated Orphans

Ann Kliman and Gilbert Kliman

A thoroughgoing demonstration of childhood bereavement as a causal factor in emotional illness requires immediate and followup studies of orphans. Thus far, only retrospective studies have been available, although these provide strongly suggestive evidence of the role bereavement plays in later adult-life emotional disorders. The Center's immediate and anterospective work with bereaved families is part of two related traditions which have recently arisen in psychiatry: the tradition of predictive longitudinal studies, and that of prevention.

There is generally insufficient medical attention to preventive measures in the midst of our busy, very hard working current-illness oriented medical world. Other more profound factors hinder investigations concerning children's reactions to death. One major obstacle to research is the general desire of adults to shield youngsters from discussions of painful events. The hope is that when children are not confronted with facts they will not be disturbed by them. It is specifically not easy to explore children's grief in a medical setting. A recent preventive psychiatry congress reported a consensus that the medical profession does not have much motivation for preventive

* *Ibid.,* Vol. 1, p. 212.

work in psychiatric areas. Several efforts by the authors and colleagues to study healthy bereaved children within routine medical channels at The Albert Einstein College of Medicine were not effective. The deliberate seeking-out of recently bereaved families to provide data on their experiences gave some indications of the difficulties which ultimately must be overcome if preventive work in this field is to attain more than token goals.

Professional resistances to work with recently bereaved families are strong. A psychoanalytically-oriented colleague who is dedicated to scientific pursuits told the authors that if he were persuaded to become involved personally in this project we would have to expect some "murder" coming from his direction. Other less self-aware professional collaborators have refused to put us in touch with bereaved families, on rationalized bases. A gynecologist was initially resistant on the basis that he could not bear to think of putting a bereaved father through "the ordeal" of talking about his experience just after his wife had died. More commonly, intellectual understanding is expressed, followed by a failure to put the team in contact with bereaved families. Perhaps some of these factors explain why so much has been written about the importance of childhood bereavement while literature on direct and prompt observation of the process is extremely scanty, to the point of near absence in the area of well children.

Another interesting reaction was that of a very honest child psychiatrist who met the authors for the first time at an orientation program for The Albert Einstein Child Fellows concerning work with disturbed bereaved children. After an hour-and-a-half meeting he had lunch with us and confided, "You know, I saw you and your wife and I was horrified. What is a nice pair like you being a couple of ghouls for? It was only later that I began to understand . . . a lot of value in the work. At first all I saw was revulsion."

As in other inquiries, the investigator's own resistances may be more hidden than those of his subjects and sources. However, there was no trouble identifying the pain caused the investigator in the process of interviewing a recently bereaved peer. The authors also found themselves particularly anxious when approaching the newly bereaved subjects. The recency of bereavement and degree of horror of surrounding circumstances had direct correlation with the degree of anxiety experienced. Upon receiving an urgent call from a colleague whose next-door neighbor had just suffered the loss of his wife and oldest son in a fire, the responding therapist missed a highway exit, causing a ten-minute delay in meeting the distraught, bereaved father of two surviving girls.

Complicated and serious resistances to research and treatment occur on the part of bereaved persons themselves. These resistances can be most unpleasant to encounter without considerable self-preparation. Many bereaved subjects were initially eager to talk. Others, however, displayed initial hostility which was in part a plea for concern and an important outlet for the rage suffered upon abandonment through death. The very perception of such hostile attitudes may be an important basis for professional resistance to early referral of bereaved persons. It is fairly well known how much hostility is anticipated by physicians approaching bereaved families for autopsy permission. Even without such requests, physicians are particularly liable to be targets of familial hostility after a death. For such reasons it is wise to remove a preventively-oriented project from the environment of a hospital, from connotations of having failed to prevent the death.

Partly by virtue of their separation from the medical profession, more ease of collaboration is provided by school teachers, clergymen, and personal friends of the bereaved family. Such contacts introduced us to all but one of the families included in the following study. The on-going constructive relationship of the contacting person to the family also influenced the ultimate outcome of investigation in terms of continuing subject availability and cooperation. In the one case where the hospital was a means of contact, the surviving parent refused followup interviews after an initially warm contact. Similarly, another family known through a cancer-detection clinic refused contact for followup after a predeath interview. As in other preventive work, special lay routes of referral were fruitful—including an organization called Parents Without Partners.

Through these unsystematic means of referral, information was gathered concerning 18 "nonpatient" children in seven recently bereaved families. Interviews concerning sixteen of the children were conducted by Ann Kliman, and those concerning two of the children by G. Kliman. The children ranged in age from less than one year to 14 years. The interval between bereavement and first contact with the surviving parent was extremely varied. It ranged from 24 hours to 15 months. The mean interval was 8 months. Efforts to reduce the mean interval between bereavement and first contact were resisted (although this picture changed when treatment services were offered). Of the seven families who provided data concerning their nineteen children, one child was excluded from the study because he already required psychiatric treatment. (Reference will be made to him because his response was of some interest.) There were eight maternal orphans and ten paternal orphans. Opposite-sex parental bereavement was the condition of six children, and same-sex parental bereavement the condition of twelve children.

Our study of these families was conducted at first through the seven surviving parents. Interviews with the surviving parent were conducted in a partially standardized fashion. The initial interview was open to whatever structure the parent wished to give it, but at some point data was obtained on about 300 items which could later be coded and rated for use in matching with a control sample and for predictive purposes. At least two hours, and often four hours, were required to gain the basic data from each surviving parent.

The participating families, with one exception, came from a comfortable Eastern metropolitan suburb. One family with three children was of an upper socioeconomic level. Four families with a total of twelve children were upper-middle class, and two families with a total of three children were lower middle-class level. The one low socioeconomic-level family studied failed to participate long enough to provide baseline data of the type we required. (It is expected that persons of low socioeconomic levels will be difficult to engage in such research.) The occupations of heads of participating families included: dentist, owner of a small creative business, two public school teachers, one research biochemist, mental hospital patient (chronically unemployed for five years), and one salesman (too physically ill to work for the past five years). The family which dropped out of our study included five children of a laborer who died of lung carcinoma. Religious categories were: Catholic, two families; Jewish, three; Protestant, three. Three, eight and seven children, respectively, were contained in each religious group. Two children were Negro, and sixteen were white.

The circumstances of each death must be taken into account in order to understand the children's responses. One mother died together with one of her children suddenly in a fire. One father hanged himself after five years of chronic manic-depressive illness. Another father died while scuba diving. A grade-school teacher (a father) who had previously been well died while suffering a 48-hour renal shutdown in the midst of influenza. One mother died within minutes after the unanticipated rupture of an unsuspected cerebral aneurism. Another mother died within two weeks after hospitalization for a carcinoma which had kept her chronically ill but active for a year. One father died after a year's lingering illness from lymphatic leukemia; another father died after ten years of chronic illness including two years of myocardial disease.

On the Unrepresentative Nature of Our Sample

It will be a long time before one can obtain a good cross section of even a limited population. Many factors enter into the willingness of a family to participate in research. Fearfulness, distrust, concern about the bad effects of meddling with a child's emotions are consciously experienced by surviving parents. Those who are referred as subjects may have eager attitudes, or motivations such as unusual trustfulness, receptivity, or hope to receive psychotherapy. Social and economic factors related to degree of enlightenment and availability for interviewing, even baby-sitting opportunities, all may have an important part in skewing the available population. Some skewing factors were partly taken into account by deliberately trying to include lower economic level families, and by going to the home for interviews so that baby-sitting did not become an obstacle.

Findings

1. Regarding weeping soon after the death, eight children were tearful for just a few minutes on the first day (see Table 3). Four children were tearful for more than a few minutes (up to over an hour) on the first day. The other six manifested no immediate tearfulness, according to parental reports. (See also relationship between immediate weeping, age and sex.)

2. Many new symptoms arose in the eighteen children within one month of bereavement (see Table 4).

3. Seven of the eighteen children began an unprecedented custom of frequently sharing a bed with the surviving parent. This usually began quickly after the death, and tended to persist.

4. Disciplinary problems arose rapidly with four children who had lost a father.

5. Verbally expressed overt and prolonged yearning for the dead parent was present in ten cases.

6. Learning-disturbances or decline in school marks occurred in two children.

7. Rapidly forming identification of the child with the dead parent (expressed in some interests, mannerisms or other behavior readily recognized by the surviving parent) occurred in seven cases.

Among the new symptoms appearing within a month of bereavement were enuresis, marked learning disturbances, phobia of insects, excessive startling, severe inability to separate from the parent, marked hypochondriacal symptoms, conversions simulating heart disease and ulcers, and antisocial episodes. Although lacking control figures, the degree and frequency of such distress signals and major new symptoms reported in a one-month period among 18 children are remarkable. These data suggest that neurosis does frequently arise or a pre-existing neurosis is frequently exacerbated upon the death of a parent. It appears especially likely that a child is suddenly disturbed when the death is sudden. Thus our data tend

TABLE 3—*Eighteen Untreated Orphans: Duration of Weeping*

		First Day		
Age at Bereavement	Sex	Several minutes to over an hour	Minutes	None
Under 1 year	m			
3.9	f			+
3.11	f			+
4.0	f		+	
4.9	f			+
5	m			+
5.5	f		+	
6	f		+	
6.6	m		+	
7.1	f		+	
8	f			+
8	m		+	
8.11	m		+	
10.7	m	+		
11	m	+		
11	m	+		
11.1	m		+	
14.3	m		+	

to confirm the retrospective analytic work of Remus-Araico (1964) and Fleming (1963).

An interesting difference appears between children who suffer an opposite-sex parental bereavement and those who suffer a same-sex bereavement. The opposite-sex children uniformly have prolonged periods of verbal expression of yearning for the lost parent. Six out of six opposite-sex children showed such expression. This phenomenon is much less frequent among the same-sex bereaved children (only three of twelve cases). Perhaps the distinction can be understood partly in terms of the sexual-object loss problem of the opposite-sex children.

TABLE 4—*Old and New Neurotic Symptoms in Eighteen Orphans within One Month after Bereavement Restricted to a List of 14 Symptoms*

	Continuing Old Symptom	New Symptom
Fearfulness	1	10
Separation difficulty	2	6
Difficulty falling asleep	0	6
Eating disturbance	1	4
Thumbsucking	3	1
Frequent bodily complaints	1	2
Frequent nightmares	0	2
Nail-biting	3	1
Stuttering	0	0
Sleepwalking	0	0
Picking at skin	1	0
Teeth grinding	0	1
Destructive	0	2
Enuretic after 4 years of age	2	1
Total number of instances of symptoms in above list prior to bereavement	14	
Total number of instances of symptoms in above list within one month after bereavement (new symptoms only)	36	
Total postbereavement symptoms	50	
Average prebereavement	0.8	
Postbereavement	2.8	
Percentage increase in symptom incidence, approximately	350%	

Prior to bereavement, the average child in the series had 0.8 or 14 symptoms listed (14 symptoms per 18 children). Within one month following bereavement, there were no instances reported of pre-existing symptoms having disappeared. On the other hand, there were 36 additional symptoms added to the group's pre-existing total. Thus the 18 children had a total of 50 symptoms, or an average of 2.8 symptoms per child, tripling the prebereavement incidence.

Other tendencies which should be considered subject to future scrutiny with larger numbers of cases are disciplinary problems and school disturbances. Thus far, they have appeared in six cases of paternal orphans but not in maternal orphans. It is doubtful that trend will hold with larger numbers and with more adolescents.

The children in our series have been rated as having excellent, good, fair or poor emotional health, according to the 300 items baseline data. The eight children with the poorest ratings turned out to be the youngest—girls whose mothers had died, and adolescent boys suffering a paternal death. Those in our series with good adjustment tended to be the oldest or to have experienced paternal bereavement just before adolescence, or were boys suffering from maternal death (even though the same family contained a poorly adjusted girl suffering the same bereavement).

Such immediate post bereavement patterns of adaptation and maladaptation should be intensively reviewed by more rigorous methods. They are quite similar to a number of large-scale retrospective studies. If our findings hold true, considerable preventive advantages could result. The case-finding problem for preventive purposes would be reduced. Preventive efforts could focus on girls suffering maternal death prior to age eight, children of very low age suffering either-sex parental death, and adolescent boys suffering paternal death. What must be done next is a study with the clinical rating process conducted in a double-blind style by people not involved in the interviewing. The reliability of the rating process must also be studied.

Much inference is required at this point to depart from the readily discerned surface phenomena of this study. Only a few aspects can be ventured here. Persistent expressions of disbelief concerning death are especially noteworthy as a possible prognostic sign, according to the age of the child. (Persistent expressions of disbelief are not equated here with a treasured fantasy that the lost parent is still alive somewhere or with the difficulty preschool children have in comprehending that death is permanent.) Among the nonpatients about whom we have data, persistent overt disbelief in the fact of death is rare. Yet among psychotic children we note [among our own patients and from Loretta Bender's reports (1954)] that very persistent disbelief in the death is overtly expressed. This may reflect the generally poor reality-testing ability of psychotic children and their susceptibility to the appearance of wish-fulfilling hallucinations.

The phenomenon of disbelief is by no means a simple one. [In response to the much less personal loss involved in President Kennedy's death, even apparently well children of all school ages had marked feelings of disbelief. (Wolfenstein and Kliman, 1965). The disbelief response persisted overtly among adolescents for weeks and months, as it did among many adults.] Open disbelief of death was seen only for a week or so among the 18 orphans in our study and for the most part only when a parent died abruptly. It was relatively strong in two sisters ages eight and six. After witnessing the death of their mother from an unsuspected cerebral aneurism, they manifested repeated profound expressions of disbelief for an entire week. An eleven-year-old boy in the same family did not personally witness the death. He had expressed disbelief less overtly but spontaneously referred to it when interviewed a half year later. He then said it had lasted a week.

Some preliminary information about the "birth" of guilt concerning parental bereavement should be presented here. Three children indicated a strong likelihood that they were elaborating guilty feelings concerning recent deaths. Douglas, even when his father died, said shortly after the death, that he and his mother were "a lot better off." He explained he was referring to financial difficulties. He had often been told during his father's illness such things as: "You're killing your father—be quiet—you upset your father—he had to lie down and take tranquilizers." Douglas openly hoped for and now still remembered hoping for his father's death. He rationalized the hope on the basis that the father would then be out of his misery. When the father died of a coronary occlusion the boy began sharing his mother's bedroom (and bed) quite regularly. He also manifested pathologic identification with his father, simulating the father's heart attacks to a frightening degree. He had other bodily concerns and abdominal pains which the father had suffered for many years. His conflict over loss and oedipal triumph was manifested through restlessness, defiant behavior, difficulty in falling asleep, increased nail-biting, and learning inhibition, as well as hypochondriasis. Douglas' response to the death of President Kennedy six months later clearly showed the influence of a guilty attitude. On the night following the President's death, the boy dreamt he was Oswald shooting the President. This was followed on the same night by a dream that he was the President being shot by Oswald. Perhaps Douglas regarded himself both as the killer of his father and the victim-father with whom he so dramatically identified somatically.

Another child in our series who appeared to suffer guilty feelings was Georgia, who was not yet four at the time of her father's death, possibly a suicide after a six-month depressive illness. Following her father's mysterious drowning in a scuba dive, Georgia became much naughtier than usual and often got into bed with her mother. She missed her father, found difficulty eating without him, and talked a great deal of him. She became increasingly hypochondriacal, which appeared to be not only a sign of depression but also an identification with the father's depressed hypochondriacal behavior in his final months. Her symptomatic headaches had also been his symptom. The couch on which she reclined, sucking her thumb in a blanket, was the couch onto which the father often withdrew on brooding silence. Georgia knew she was "responsible" for family arguments and probably suffered interference in her mourning because of her guilt. Her postbereavement naughtiness served to bring about increased punishments.

The third probably guilt-burdened child in our series was Thomas, age sixteen years, who had been "excluded" from the series because he was already emotionally ill at the time of his father's death by suicide. Thomas had previously witnessed a suicide attempt by his father and had talked the father out of it when the father tried to hang himself. When the father later succeeded in hanging himself, Thomas was away at school and felt that if only he had been home he could have once more talked his father out of what he described as a cowardly act. His psychiatric treatment was resumed, but details are lacking with the exception that Thomas feared he would become insane like his father.

When a bereaved child has a tendency to guilt feelings it is not only a problem in itself but may indicate a strong set of unhealthy processes already at work for a long time prior to the bereavement. We cannot be primarily concerned here about the pre-existing problems. Our aims in pursuing this study included making predictions as to which children would require help in the near- and long-range future. To that end we recorded our interviews in a codifiable manner. Hopefully, there are predictive items in our study which will be correlated with future pathology that we may explore with statistical analysis. But this aspect of the work has only been prepared rather than carried into action and therefore cannot be usefully pursued here.

Further Notes on Childhood Bereavement

The reader may rightfully complain that the preceding sparse account is inadequate to describe the psychological emergencies suffered by the eighteen untreated orphans. Certainly the small group psychology of the family and in particular the influence of parental mourning upon childhood mourning have been slighted in this presentation. The use of children as proxies for denial and avoidance of painful memories and emerging affects has not been well delineated. The passionate relationships which arise between the bereaved generations through argument and through frank eroticism have been insufficiently noted. But perhaps the reader can sense the fateful and far from pallid means with which children confront parental death, and will share with the author a feeling for the multiple human necessities and opportunities which exist in this still largely uncharted area of human psychology. Some consideration will now be given to one especially neglected area—psychological economy in mourning.

In *Mourning and Melancholia* (1917) Freud comments upon the extreme psychological pain which follows death of a love-object. He attributes this experience of pain to the necessity for recognizing that the object no longer exists in external reality. It may be useful to go beyond this view and postulate that another process is also at work which is consequent upon the nonexistence of the love-object in external reality. So long as a spouse, sibling, or a young child's parent exists as an object of frequent perception in external reality, there are seldom any intrusions of that mental representation into daytime psychic life in the form of hallucinations, hypnogogic experiences, or pressing memories. Yet, in conditions of separation or bereavement, it is very frequently noted that the absent object appears pressingly in memories (often of an involuntary sort). It has also been noted in our own series and Marris's (1958) that presumably healthy widows and bereaved children experience hallucinations and illusions regarding the dead person. An oppressive, implacable quality of nighttime hypnogogic occupations with thoughts about the lost object is also frequent in bereaved persons.

A question may be raised as to whether these hallucinatory, hypnagogic, and obsessive memory processes are all the result of yearnings. In addition, conflicts concerning former aggressive impulses directed at the absent or deceased object still leave the formulation incomplete. The question of the economic or energic effect of realistic perception should be included in order that a more complete understanding be reached. The lack of external stimulation in the darkness of an empty bedroom is an energic consideration. Under these circumstances there are not only special sexual and aggressive inclinations toward the absent object, there is also a distinct lack of substitutive stimuli.

It seems useful to think of an economic equilibrium between the externally perceived real object and the stored mental representations of that object. The memories or mental representations of the object are charged. It is proposed that, as long as excitation of energy occurs within the organism as a fresh response to an externally perceived love-object, there is no call upon the accumulated investment of libidinal and aggressive energy with which the memories of the object are charged. However, when the external object by its absence fails to stimulate the excitement and discharge process, then the internalized object is called upon to play the same role in the psychological economy. In order to play the role formerly occupied by an externally perceived object, the internal mental representation must operate with some of the energy it has accumulated through former investment. If this process is very energetic or occurs under circumstances where reality-testing is diminished (such as states of great wishfulness, fatigue, toxicity or sleep), then the internal excitations released may reach the level of hallucination.

The process of regression is also partly a psychological economy measure, common in the response and adaptation of children to any emergency. Here the concept of regression is used in a rather literal fashion: the turning back of psychological development to earlier stages of adaptation. Thus, the relatively disorganized child under stress may temporarily function with modes of energy distribution less complex than he utilizes when not under stress.

The concept is one which is quite faulty in its theoretical elucidation at this time, and thorough understanding of regression may ultimately involve the use of concepts related to entropy. There is a tendency for any complex system (including living organisms and physical chemical systems) to lapse in to a state of lesser complexity of organization when damaged. The concept of entropy or an entropy-like process is useful in a heuristic fashion, when taking in to consideration that the maintenance of psychological defensive systems is not only a matter of psychological economy, but also requires energy expenditure for maintenance of defenses. Thus, for example, the defense of repression, which can function against incestuous desires, requires energy to maintain, although it also spares the expenditure of energy which comes from distress when incestuous impulses emerge into consciousness. An external situation such as seduction or rape by a parent, or increased proximity to an opposite-sex parent after same-sex bereavement may cause the child to forcefully become aware of his own sexual feelings in regard to the incestuous object. Then he must utilize increased amounts of psychological energy in order to maintain or reinstitute the defense of repression. Under these circumstances, return to a more elementary level of psychological function in which repression is not emphasized or even used may be economical. Thus, a psychotic state in a child subjected to abrupt bereavement or incestuous rape could be an entropy-like response.

It should be kept in mind that less gross and less entropy-like regressions in states of stress can also be adaptive in transient and flexible ways. Such regressions resemble "regressions in the service of the ego," seen in healthier states. The regression of a frightened child who must be cuddled or even slept with as if he were once more a baby can be a means for acquiring short-term increases of psychosocial sustenance, or valuable in restoring more stable uses of psychological energy in a short period of time.

On the Adequacy of Childhood Mourning

With regard to the question of how far children's mourning differs phenomenologically from that of adults, our study suggests that the differences are more matters of degree than quality.

The work of mourning can be divided conveniently into three areas for consideration in respect to developmental differences: (1) testing and accepting the reality of the loss; (2) remembering—working over and decathecting the memories concerning the lost object; (3) cultivating substitute object relationships. A good deal of mourning work in all three areas can be expected of a healthy child. A marked lack of or extremely intense work may be poor prognostic signs.

Testing the reality of parental death may be very difficult. A six-year-old girl whose mother died abruptly of cerebral hemorrhage would frequently imagine that her mother was sitting on her bed in the morning. The fantasy consisted of her mother talking to her quietly, apparently very close to a memory of real events. It was an incomplete mourning process as long as it retained an almost hallucinatory vigor, the gratifying memories being difficult to surrender to the forces of reality. The child's experiences resemble those reported by Marris (1958) as being regular occurrences among widows in the first few years of bereavement.

Some children in our study enjoyed reminiscing about their dead parents. Two young adolescent boys watched home movies over and over, on their own initiative, and seemed to enjoy the process of observing their dead father in the films. Two other boys (ages nine and seven) learned to run the projector themselves because their mother was not in accord with this process of working over memories with photographic assistance. The mother's interference with this process, although not strong, is indicative of how adults can stop or mask children's mourning work. One family illustrated this point with special clarity. The father felt guilt-stricken because he had not saved his wife and son from a fire, and actually made a compact between his two daughters and himself that they would not mention their mother in his presence. If they did so, he would cry, which was considered undesirable by all. In this fashion the father may have implied to his children that the work of mourning was too painful for human endurance.

One form of mourning work in childhood is the playing-out of fantasies concerning activities characteristic of the dead parent. Occasionally this remembering activity may contribute to identification with the dead and increasingly idealized lost object. This appeared to be the case with Hilda, whose school-teacher father died abruptly and unexpectedly of renal shutdown during influenza. A year following her father's death she continued a rapidly initiated custom of pretending to be a school teacher. The game appeared socially important and was a regular part of her peer games. A more solitary closeness to her father may have been in her continued and expanded interest in his hobby of gardening. Four-year-old Donna exhibited her "memorial" work by quickly increasing avidity for her talented mother's artistic activities. She soon became proficient considerably beyond her years at sketching and painting. This process was clearly an effort to replace, as well as remember, her mother, since she assured her father that he "shouldn't worry because" she would "be a mommy soon." In addition to their oedipal aspects, her artistic activities enabled Donna to think about her mother in the play-identification fashion appropriate to her age.

The most important phase of mourning, however, is that of recovery, accompanied by increased ability to invest libido in new objects. This phase is certainly evident in childhood, and sometimes is vigorous quite soon. The younger children in our study appeared less inhibited than older children in seeking new objects of the same sex as the dead parent. In early adolescents and older children the process occasionally seemed impeded. Problems of loyalty conflicts confront latency and adolescent children quite forcefully. They may become quarrelsome members of the family when the surviving parent approaches remarriage.

Assessing a Child's Need for Preventive Intervention

All signs point to caution when considering the mourning work of a child to be adequate, no matter how good the immediate clinical situation. No doubt the majority of bereaved children will grow up free of major emotional disorders. Yet we cannot improve with any certainty upon the predicament of an eminent child psychoanalyst who examined a five-year-old bereaved boy about twenty years ago. At that time the child's mother requested evaluation of the child since there had been a terrible experience. The father had stabbed the mother and child quite viciously and then jumped out a window to his own death, in the child's presence. The mother was scarred across the chest and back, as was the boy. Yet the child's clinical condition was good. Some twelve years later the boy became psychotic and suicidal. He apparently could not bear separation from his mother upon going to college, combined with the symbolic oedipal triumph of the academic success he was beginning to experience (Wilder, 1959).

A combination of statistical, clinical, theoretical and common-sense factors leads to the proposal of the following criteria for preventive intervention following childhood bereavement.

Even in the absence of signs and symptoms of childhood psychiatric illness, any *one* of the following make preventive intervention desirable whether or not there is any other factor present:

1. Suicide as a cause of a parent's death.
2. Very poor relationship between child and dead parent.
3. Very poor relationship between child and surviving parent.
4. Dead parent was mentally ill and living with the family during the year prior to death.
5. Remaining parent mentally ill.
6. Maternal bereavement of a girl less than eight years old.

Any *two* of the following factors make preventive intervention desirable:

7. Age less than four years at bereavement.
8. Child at one time having had a neurotic or psychotic illness.
9. Paternal death during a boy's adolescence.
10. Death forces a geographic move or causes severe economic hardship.
11. No readily available substitute object of same sex and appropriate age.
12. Remaining parent has pathologic mourning.
13. Remaining parent has increasing physical intimacy with child.
14. Child over age eight years old sheds no tears in first weeks after death.
15. Child over age four does not discuss dead parent or fact of death.
16. Child over age five refuses to participate in family funeral or religious observances.
17. Child has unusually cheerful mood beginning first week after parent's death.
18. Death was abrupt and unexpected.
19. Terminal illness was more than six months.
20. The terminal illness was unusually disfiguring, or involved mental deterioration or physical mutilation.
21. Death from childbirth, uterine, ovarian or breast carcinoma if child is girl.

22. Family did not explain illness to child or deliberately concealed illness.
23. Family delayed informing child of death when others knew, for more than one day.

On Advising Parents

The recent trend in our culture includes some pretenses that ugliness, disfigurement and death are unreal. This denial of reality is displaced by us unto our children, whom we hope will become islands of comfort and innocence. No matter how protective it may seem, such deception sets a dangerous model for the child is his own adaptations to harsh facts.

There is much value in tactful but deliberate education and preparation of children for a death in the family. Death is much more common that we wish to believe, even in the circle of acquaintances and relatives of small children. There is an immunizing value therefore in seizing any opportunity to discuss and expose a child to the fact of death of animals. He should be helped to understand at a very early age that animals stop breathing, eating, defecating, die and are buried. This will give him an opportunity to ask and have his questions answered in an area of relatively low emotional investment.

It should be made clear to parents that bereavement is by no means a sufficient cause to produce mental illness and that the majority of bereaved adults and children do very well. Outstanding examples of persons orphaned early in their lives who have had productive existences are Abraham Lincoln and Harriet Beecher Stowe, to cite only two.

Concerning the religious aspects of children's reactions to death, sometimes families are very disorganized intellectually following a death and have difficulty explaining their own beliefs to a child—even when they would ordinarily be capable of making a clear statement. For such a family, a clergyman can be of utmost help if he is asked to make a special effort with the children. Unless a clergyman is invited to help he may be hesitant to invade the child's psychological privacy and may spend most of his time with the adults. However, the calm and experience of a clergyman, who by profession is accustomed to death and oriented to thinking of it as a natural part of God's intentions, can convey to the children some of the same kind of strength which is desirable for the surviving parent to convey. The clergyman may thus become a model, and to some extent a substitute for a missing parent, someone to whom the child can regularly turn for support and explanation.

Regarding age differences, parents need to know that a child may be too immature to grasp the concept of death and its finality. However, he is not too young to perceive and react to the fact that a family member is absent. Even a young infant suffers from the loss of his mother—responding with changes of eating and digestive processes. Age differences are very marked, and parents should know that young children cannot grieve openly for more than brief periods.

In regard to the stages of childhood mourning, advice given to families should be certain not to equate mourning with grieving. Mourning is a healing process which may go on silently. Anger, guilt and anxiety are regular parts of mourning. Also among the components of mourning are the powerful emotions of *grief* and *protest*. These emotions are excited by the action of a part of the mind which recognizes reality and demands that the mourner must admit he has lost the loved person. Only when reality is recognized, however dimly, can there be painful emotions. *Despair* is an emotion of mourning which, if prolonged, may require professional help to overcome. Yet it occurs regularly in adult grief. It is usually absent as an observable emotion in childhood. Children feel the emotion of guilt even more intensely if they happen to be young enough to imagine they are magically responsible for the person's death. *Reorganization* eventually occurs in adults and children and it includes the establishment of new love relationships as well as giving up the realistic tie to the lost one. A curious stage of mourning, not widely recognized, is that of *identification with the lost person.* It is an unconscious and often constructive process. It can, however, become harmful under certain circumstances. For example, literal taking of the parent's place should be discouraged. This is another reason why sharing of the surviving parent's bed should be tactfully avoided. Constructive outcomes of identification include the development of certain strengths which become independent, such as the acquisition of hobbies, interest and skills which were characteristic of the deceased parent or sibling. These should be encouraged and sometimes overtly recognized as the sign of the child's love and desire to be close to the lost parent, but there is no special reason to dwell verbally upon the child's effort to master his loss through identification.

Concerning the unfortunate effects of euphemisms comparing death to sleep, children often become afraid to fall asleep, thinking that it is literally an introduction to death. Doctors are familiar with a similar problem when parents have equated general anesthesia with falling asleep—that children are not only disillusioned but inclined to be frightened about falling asleep thereafter.

When parents ask how much a child should participate in funerals and burials, beyond verbal explanations sometimes the best explanation for a child is to share and observe certain procedures. For example, it is helpful to many children that they are not only "told" that the dead person is buried, but are allowed to "see" for themselves. Children old enough to ask the question, "What happens to Daddy now?" will have less active fantasies if they literally see that their father is buried. There is a tendency for children between three and ten to invent elaborate resurrection fantasies. Often a child who has not seen the burial will even believe that the parent has gone on a trip to another state and will some day suddenly reappear. Grownups who themselves are disposed to such hopeful fantasies at least have the benefit of a strong sense of reality to contradict their hopes. A child's sense of reality is often so frail that real observation of the burial is useful.

Parents can facilitate childhood mourning. Among the specific ways, is in placing special emphasis on that aspect of mourning which requires remembering. It is quite difficult for most children to go through the bit by bit remembering and feeling about the memories which is a necessary part of successful mourning. The sense of reality about the death having actually taken place is frail and the challenge presented by remembering is often avoided. If an adult will lend his strength by gently and affectionately discussing facts about the parent, episodes, characteristics, or special qualities of the parent's life, a child (of almost any age) will benefit. A surviving parent, close friend or relative can also help a child occasionally remember unpleasant factors in his relationship with the dead parent and unpleasant features of the dead parent's behavior. This is a very valuable assistance in releasing the resentments which are a natural part of every child's store of feelings regarding a parent. At all times, however, adults must remember the concept of "dosage." What may seem like a perfectly acceptable amount of remembering loving or resenting may be much too large for a given child at a given age. Parents should be advised to try to think of how different in size a pediatric aspirin is from a growup's aspirin, and how upset a child's stomach might be if he took four grownup aspirins at once. Mourning is an even more bitter medicine.

There is a distinct lack of synchrony between the generations in the rhythms of grief and the other processes of mourning. The latency child, who in the first week after his parent's death can freely bicycle, roller skate, and play ball at a time when his family is shrouded in the blackest grief, may nevertheless be bitterly loyal to the same deceased parent when years later the time comes for remarriage. Beneath the surface, completely out of step with the rest of his family, the child is still mourning. A respect for this difference in timing is the first step in preventing it from becoming an obstacle in family harmony.

Guidelines for Parents Concerning When Psychotherapy Is Needed

1. When a child shows signs of "regression" for more than a few weeks.

2. When a new symptom occurs. Separation and sleep problems are common. A particularly frequent and particularly obstinate symptom following bereavement is a prolonged decline in school marks. This could reflect a dread of knowledge, an anxiety about ambitions, or lack of love for life.

3. Suicidal threats are more common among bereaved children than the general population and should be taken more seriously as they contain an element of an urge for a reunion with the lost parent.

4. Dissatisfaction with the child's own sexual identity should also be taken seriously. If a bereaved boy or girl expresses a strong desire to be of the opposite sex, this is more significant than it ordinarily would be, although such statements are widespread before school age. The difficulty should be considered important no matter which parent has died.

5. The tendency to stay home from school should be interrupted quickly with psychotherapy.

6. Sexual promiscuity may be an escape from new intimacy with the surviving parent. It is very difficult to distinguish between normal sexual pressures of adolescence and the special problems likely to occur among bereaved children. The best advice for bereaved families is "when in doubt, consult."

Advice for bereaved families should be optimistic in most cases. The themes of crisis mastery and new steps in personal identity formations can be merged with the theme of construction identifications with the lost object. A helpful concept for bereaved mothers is Hilgard's view of the strong widow as a valuable model and support for her family. Hilgard's research concerning long-range effects of childhood bereavement shows that a widow who is literally strong and supports her family often has the pleasure of seeing a good psychological outcome for her children. A mother who can quickly resume work or take a job in order to replace her husband's economic role in the family apparently does not deprive her children of her emotional strength. Instead she provides them with an example of behavior which proves that life goes on and that it can go on vigorously (Hilgard, 1960).

Notes on the Constructive Outcome of Bereavement

At times socially useful consequences appear to flow from parental death. Roe (1953) studied a group of outstanding biologists, finding that 25 per cent of them had lost a parent by death before age ten. Gregory (1965) in his study of 1700 Carleton College students reported that of four male and three female students who graduated summa cum laude, two of the male students had lost a parent by death. Gregory believes that factors associated with bereavement may lead some students to strive for exceptional achievement. It will take long anterospective work before it can be said with any certainty which of the various types of childhood mourning have a favorable or unfavorable outcome. That the outcome can be favorable should not be doubted. The vast majority of bereaved children will function quite adequately although the degree of covert pathology has never been systematically estimated.

One of the more floridly speculative hopes which might be entertained for the distant future is that the influence of object-loss on character formation can be systematically and advantageously understood. The shadow of the lost object appears to be falling clearly upon the developing ego of the bereaved child. Fantasies and memories concerning the dead parent appear to help rather precipitously, if not prematurely, crystallize certain features of the child's character development. The fact that such an influence needs to be encouraged in some instances as a form of mourning or to be alleviated in others as a form of pathologic identification may be an area of crucial decision for preventive work.

CHAPTER IV

Divorce and Marital Separation

A TANTALIZING QUALITY exists about the loss and separation problems in divorce. In a death, the child's perception of reality begins to tell him that the lost parent does not return. But in a divorce, his perception of reality tells him there is at least some possibility of the parent returning. This realistic hope may be bitterly frustrated. Because yearnings to reunite with the lost parent are seldom given up, children have more difficulty in grasping other realities of divorce, such as the acquisition of new children by the "lost" parent.

Age differences in children's reactions to divorce are necessarily very marked. It is doubtful whether a child under age four can understand the concept of permanence. Therefore he cannot really understand that his parents will not be living together. His grasp extends for a few days or weeks at a time. In his early school years he will understand concepts of months and even years. But the idea of an endless or permanent arrangement is not truly comprehensible until he reaches age eight to ten.

Children of preschool years will have the strongest need for assurance that at least one parent will take care of them. The separation from one parent arouses dread that the other parent will also leave the child. By age five or six, a child is usually able to understand that he has not actually been abandoned.

An important reverberation with adolescent development is that teenagers will worry about their own marital future. They need explanation that children do not always repeat the mistakes and unhappiness of their own parents, and, moreover, that children can even learn from the mistakes of their parents.

The younger a child is (providing he is able to talk sentences), the more likely he is to have magical feelings about his own powers. He may believe that angry wishes have actually made a parent go away. Often, children correctly believe that they have caused parents to argue. A child may have enjoyed provoking disputes between his parents. In such a family it is important that a child be helped to understand that he has really been a part of the family quarreling, but that the quarrels over his own behavior were not as important as he thought. He should be told that there were other more important quarrels that he did not have anything to do with, and that grownups have some strong feelings about each other which have nothing to do with their feelings about their children.

Among difficulties produced for children in families where one parent is verbally degraded by the other, is the sense of degradation a child feels regarding his own identity. To the extent that he feels himself to be like the reproached parent, a child is liable to reproach himself as worthless or someone to be hated. If this feeling becomes associated with his sexual identity, it may become difficult for a child to be comfortable with his own sexual development. For these reasons and others, it is of the utmost importance that children not be used as audiences and pawns in postdivorce (or predivorce) efforts to destroy a parent's image.

But there is no point in avoiding discussion of what the child can perceive about either parent's behavior. For example, if the child has reason to know that the father does not pay the required alimony, or knows that for several weeks the checks have been withheld, it is important to acknowledge this perception. Similarly, if either parent has filled the child with reproachful accounts of the former spouse's behavior, there is much to be gained by allowing the child to repeat what he has heard. At least one parent can help by listening and not compounding reproaches with more reproaches. What is important is that the child should be kept out of the role of being a pawn. Just as in bereavement, he can tolerate adult expressions of emotion—even of hatred. But he cannot tolerate very well the misuse of his childhood yearnings and attachments by efforts to involve him in a hateful transaction.

A child who is fairly stable emotionally will find relationships in his ordinary life which help compensate for the loss of one parent or another. For example, a boy living in a fatherless home will become more attached to male teachers, counselors, clergymen, or recreation supervisors than other boys. These relationships can be extremely constructive and, when supervised well, are to be encouraged.

Some positive, constructive actions which most parents can take include making it clear to the children that they very definitely have a continuing family life. Numerous previously observed family rituals and customs should be underlined to give the children a sense of continuity. Events such as Thanksgiving and Christmas celebrations can be prepared for weeks and months in advance to help recognize that even without father or mother in the house the essential spirit of celebration continues, and that a number of relatives from outside the immediate family home are still part of their lives. Contacts with adult friends on the same basis are also valuable. Expansion of family social interests may have a very useful function.

There is a special organization called "Parents without Partners" which has this expansion as its main goal. Whether or not this particular organization exists in a given community, its functions might be attained by a determined parent. These include many social activities in which partnerless parents can meet and provide each other with companionship. Adults from the organization function as big brothers and big sisters or substitute fathers and mothers for social occasions such as outings and expeditions. Parents Without Partners also has a program of parent-guidance lectures and seminars run by invited experts.

The "Big Brother" organization makes a special point of recognizing the need of fatherless boys for masculine guidance and companionship. The community appears to pay less attention to the needs of fatherless girls and also tends to ignore the possibility of helping motherless boys and girls within their own families. However, family service agencies in any community can be contacted for assistance with these matters.

Divorced children have many problems which strongly resemble those of bereaved children. For example, children of both sexes are inclined to share a parental bed following a divorce or bereavement. It is important to understand this as coming as much from the loneliness of the parent as from the loneliness of the child. Only when the parent recognizes that he, too, wants an extra companionship will the problem cease. Little girls are inclined to become unduly housewifely in the absence of a mother. Little boys are apt to become unduly bossy and take on "the man in the house" behavior, not entirely to the distaste of their divorced mothers, who may be unconsciously yearning to have a man in the house. When such behavior becomes extreme, guidance should be sought from the pediatrician who may recommend psychological treatment to prevent further difficulties.

Quarrelsomeness of children in divorced families may develop for a variety of reasons. It appears in all combinations of boy-mother, boy-father, girl-mother, and girl-father twosomes. It seems to have a defensive purpose, preventing affectionate relationships which are unconsciously disturbing to the people involved. In other words, a risk develops because there are now unattached feelings which tend to settle in an inappropriate way into the parent-child relationship. It is thus important for parents to respect the childish quality of their own children, and not demand from their children expressions or relationships which would be more appropriate from an adult—such as physical closeness, advice, sharing intimacies about marital difficulties, or sharing intimacies about new social experiences.

The best preventive work a parent can do with a child when a divorce is impending to let the child know as soon as possible what the expected reality will be. According to each child's age and ability to understand, some of the reasons for the divorce should be explained a long time in advance. This gives the child a chance to vent his resentment against the still-present parent who later will not be readily available for such direct expression or with whom the child may be later more reluctant to speak frankly without the protection of both parents being present.

Regarding marital separations of any kind, most long separations from a parent are predictable, and many of them have a predictably unpleasant quality for which the child should be prepared. When a parent has an illness which will require months of hospitalization, there usually should be at least days or even weeks of warning. If a parent must go to jail, the family usually knows about it during court proceedings. The parent is likely to be out on bail for at least a short time before he is sentenced. If a father is in military service, generally there should be at least a few weeks in which to prepare. In all these cases, a straightforward account of the essential facts to the children is just as advisable it is regarding illness, death and divorce. Even when a father has to go to jail, the child should be told the unpleasant facts. In this case the child still suffers a social stigma, but it will not be lessened by deceiving him. The child will be better prepared if he shares with his family what they know about the facts. An exception can be made if the family is in possession of information which would damage the parent if the child revealed it. Although not sufficiently used by families of prisoners, many states have a social worker available for consultation to the prisoners and families of prisoners. Some penal systems also have a psychiatrist available for consultation, again seldom used by the families. Much remains to be learned about the problems of prison inmates' families and how better to help them.

When a parent is involuntarily or voluntarily in the military service, much of the family's emotional response will be colored by the circumstances of his service, as well as by the developmental status of the children and the emotional status of the mother. If the father has rather reluctantly and involuntarily gone to fight in a dangerous battle, the family will understandably be more frightened and probably more disorganized than if he has voluntarily enlisted with the full knowledge and encouragement of his family in what he considers to be a patriotic and urgently important battle. The military service has an excellent provision for psychiatric services for families of military dependents, and, of course, should be consulted if there is any question about the emotional well-being of the child or mother.

Principles of helping a child during periods of long separation include (as indicated in Chapter III, Death in the Family) tolerance of regressive trends. It is better to have a child to become less mature and have small regressions for a few weeks at a time than to suddenly experience a sharp, gross regression. Small regressions may prevent a child from taking more desperate measures later. One way of preventing a child from feeling desperate is to be sure he has every opportunity to visit the missing parent, regulations permitting. It is probably a mistake to think that a child will be more damaged by seeing his father in jail than imagining what a jail is like. It does him some good to have direct visual and physical contact with the father. Correspondence, phone calls, and exchange of presents are also very helpful.

CASE REPORT

The case of Theodore* illustrates a loyalty crisis which not only existed in the boy, but was also a reflection of parental ambivalence. The 13-year-old boy kept running away from and fighting with his divorced, remarried mother. He kept claiming that he wanted to live with his father, an attitude which contrasted with that of his four younger siblings.

* Treatment was given by Daniel Feinberg, M.D.

After several consultations with the mother and father, as well as with Theodore, it was found that the arrangement was mutually desired. In fact, the mother was so burdened by her own psychological problems that she had in effect arranged to evict the child by having him run away. She responded to his provocativeness with such physical abuse that a governmental agency had its attention called to the problem. Upon transfer of the child's residence to his father, there ensued a period of quiescence in which the family's ambivalences were verbalized and ventilated at a more manageable level within the interview framework rather than through real-life action.

An unfortunate feature of this case was that an extra crisis was induced into the child's life when he was required to testify against his mother in court. It is almost always advisable for such proceding to take place either in the judge's chambers, or to be kept out of court entirely if possible. Children only come to regret later in life what their childhood confusions, prejudices and susceptibilities to persuasion by adults have led them to say in court. Several instances of bad effects of such procedures have been documented by the author and colleagues at The Center for Preventive Psychiatry. Although no control for the series is available and the circumstances leading to such procedures are in themselves usually pathogenic, there is a preliminary impression that official testimony by a child against a parent is a severe burden.

Another feature of this case which deserves mention is the custody of a male child by his unmarried father. Experience in such cases is necessarily colored by the fact that the child's later love for a woman is strained by the unsatisfactory, psychotic or destructive qualities of his mother's behavior which have led to his being in the custody of his father. In addition, the enforced intimacy with the same-sex parent, unless that parent has a reliable and satisfactory sexual partner to whom the boy can become attached, will dispose the boy to inhibition of his own heterosexual development. We have witnessed the sad evolution of one such boy who went through circumstances similar to Theodore's. After ten years he was evicted by the father who could not bear the homosexual petulance and quarrelsomeness of the now-effeminate son for whose custody he had bitterly fought.

CHAPTER V

Minor Emergencies

The First Days of School

In the past few decades psychiatrists, pediatricians and educators have increasingly come to grips with a clinical syndrome called "school phobia." Of enormous complexity because it is exceedingly variable in meaning and importance depending on the individual child and circumstances under which it occurs, and because it is associated with maternal pathology, school phobia is nevertheless a matter for public health concern. Epidemiologic and preventive principles are gradually being brought to bear upon the problem.

It is lamentable, however, that the most rigorous public health measures in this instance are by no means being practiced by public authorities. In fact, it is private nursery schools and professional associations of nursery school teachers who are facing up to the problem of school phobia, while public school authorities react with the understandable lack of action which stems from the financial and psychological expenses they might incur if the problem were faced honestly.

For purposes of this discussion, school phobia may be defined as any condition in which a child attending school becomes anxious or psychosomatically upset when time comes to go to school. Often the distress fades after the child has arrived in class, but he may go to the school nurse complaining of a stomachache or headache. Or he may find means to leave the school without permission. There is a biphasic curve of frequency in which school phobia is manifested, the greatest frequencies being in the first few years of school and in the middle years of high school. The latter age group is quite difficult to treat. The earlier group is characterized by pronounced maternal pathology in the sphere of permitting the child to separate, so that treatment may often be successfully directed primarily to either mother or child or both.

Since there cannot be an exhaustive discussion here, coverage of this psychological emergency will be limited to its prevention and management of the earliest stages in young children. A model in prevention can be found in a growing number of modern nursery schools which build an understanding of separation problems into the structure of their earliest contacts with new pupils. It is strongly recommended that the pediatrician or psychiatrist consulted about a nursery school for a healthy or neurotic youngster should specify a school which carries out the following minimum preventive program.

Nursery classroom work must be preceded by

1. A formal interview between teacher and the child's parents, so the parents may convey their impressions to the child and the teacher will know the family.
2. An individual play session between the teacher and child in the otherwise empty classroom.

Once classroom work begins,

1. The mother should be present during most of the first session, and in a nearby room—available to enter the classroom—for part of several more sessions.
2. Upon the appearance of any sign of regression, marked anxiety or development of a new emotional problem, the child should have his mother in the classroom again. If the problem persists the child should be withdrawn temporarily or until the next semester, with guidance given the mother in regard to strengthening the mother-child abilities to separate from each other. The situation of inability to tolerate early nursery-school days is often the first important sign of emotional difficulties requiring psychiatric help.

More sophisticated and powerful measures are taken by some nursery schools, of which the physician or therapist may wish to be aware. There are a number of schools in which the intake procedure includes extensive history-taking, so that the school director has advance warning of the possibility that a particular child will be sensitive to separations. The author, together with Mrs. Doris Gorin and Mrs. Elissa Burian, designed a palatable questionnaire for self-administration by parents applying to nursery schools. Such a questionnaire, now in use for three years, supplements the "early-warning" system which is so essential in preventive work. Hopefully it will provide an instrument for predictive use.

Among other useful procedures now in practice by preventively-oriented nursery schools is the home-visit. Through a pre-entry home visit, the family and teachers become more friendly and a more complete picture of family life is available for the staff. The home visit is a strong facilitator of early adjustment in nursery school and has gained some acceptance among several university-directed Headstart programs where the value is especially high.

An area of especially bad practice in regard to management of early separation problems is found in most public kindergartens and most Headstart programs. With short-sighted attention to immediate economy of staff time and public funds, there is generally no teacher-parent interview in public kindergartens until after the child has been in class for several weeks—a complete reversal of desirable preventive practice, without financial justification. No home-visiting is practiced in public kindergartens, where such a proposal would generally meet with administrative dread of civic protests regarding invasion of privacy. Headstart programs which tend to more home-visiting (so far known to the author) are still not carrying out this much-needed procedure in the majority of cases. Nor is Headstart, with its great need for emotional enrichment, paying sufficient attention to the need for parental presence in the classroom in early days of work. The author suspects that Headstart children, because of their capacity to develop facades of self-sufficiency, are being treated differently in this regard than emotionally deprived children of upper-class families receiving private, intense enrichment programs. For example, there is a deplorable tendency to put Headstart children in a school bus on the first day, without parents accompanying each child. Rationalizations that working mothers cannot attend do not hold.

A point must be made that the majority of three- and four-year-old children (certainly almost all five-year-old children) are capable of adapting to the first days of school without overt regression or symptom formation. The issue at stake, however, is not only that of illness. The issue (particularly in marginal children, such as those in Headstart) is that of the maximum cultivation of human resources and potentials. Under circumstances of abrupt and unprepared separation from mothers, preschool children can adapt to the external requirements of the school situation. But the adaptation is more often on a level of strain than it should be. This strain is an obstacle to maximum development of sublimative activities such as painting, constructive play, and love for learning. Under conditions of strain, there is likely to be a tendency toward compliance with external requirements, rather than toward true love of learning. Thus, the reading readiness, which is so blatantly emphasized as a goal for culturally deprived children, is actually undermined through heedless attitudes concerning mother-child separations. All evidence collected by psychoanalytically oriented investigators of early childhood development points to an inextricable network of connections between object-love and ego-function development. Disruption of the mother-child relationship on any but the most careful basis is likely to handicap ego-function growth on the preschool level. Here, once more, principles of dosage, careful development of strength, and immunizing experiences which cultivate psychological strength are pertinent for full success in the first days of school.

The First Season of Summer Camp

Certainly most camp directors would be disappointed to find this experience listed in a work which contains discussions of serious anguish. A preventive view requires facing the fact that, although frequency of happy outcome of first summers away is high—even at ages five and six—the seriousness of regressions away from home warrants mention. Furthermore, because of selfish reasons, often well rationalized and sincerely felt, professional camp directors are in a position similar to professional administrators of pediatric wards. They are coerced by their own needs to overlook the subtle phenomena of regression and strain in children's emotional development, and inclined to look with dismay upon the influence of parental presence. Generations of needless misery passed before modern pediatric wards caught up with knowledge of children's needs for emotional closeness to their parents. Even at the tenderest ages, children were thought to be better behaved and certainly easier to manage with little or no parental visiting, despite months of separation.

For the sake of brevity, only a sketchy set of preventive recommendations will be presented as follows:

1. The child should be informed beforehand by clear evidence that his parents chose the particular camp after careful study and

upon good recommendations. Physically visiting a nearby child who has had a satisfactory experience at the camp is reassuring; indeed the reassurance which results is worth even taking a winter afternoon's trip if there is no former camper nearby.

2. No child of under six should be away from home as long as two months for the first time at camp. The child should have prior experience with being away for a week or two with persons who are well known to him. The camp season should be limited to several weeks.

3. The good practice of professional camp directors who visit the homes of new campers and tell the children about camp should be established where possible. The specific counselor for the child's bunk should visit the home before camp begins, or else correspond with the child.

4. Under age eight, parents should visit the child at camp for a weekend at least every two weeks. There is resistance from many camp directors on this issue, and such camps should be avoided, especially since even more frequent visiting is psychologically mandatory if there is evidence of regression.

5. It is desirable for a child to remain at camp even when he experiences psychological trouble which has newly developed there. He can usually master the problems with the help of frequent visiting. Emphasis should be placed on growth through surmounting the feeling of helplessness, but only if parental support is available in a tangible form. Telephone calls, photographs, and frequent letters are supportive, usually, rather than temptations to regression. It is generally undesirable for the child to return home because of separation problems unless there is evidence of a profound regression, psychotic processes, or special reasons why the child should be at home. (For example, these special reasons might include the desirability of having the child be present for a wedding, or to participate in a family mourning precipitated by a midsummer death.)

6. Unless the camp permits frequent visiting, onset of a new symptom or recurrence of one which had been absent for a year is clear indication to return the child home. Probably the most common symptoms which occur among latency and preadolescent children away from home are bed-wetting, sleep disturbances, stuttering, phobias and stealing.

Moving to a New Home

Moving may become an identity-changing experience. It need not be an identity crisis, but almost always provides a strain on the child's concept of himself and the world.

Many of the same factors which are looked forward to hopefully or with concern by adults are also important to even the youngest children. Some families have to help a child adapt to a completely alien country. Even a move into a neighborhood of different ethnic, religious, economic, or racial composition has distinct impact on most children who have reached the kindergarten or first grade level. Preventive measures include preparing the child to understand the differences in customs, practices, mores, appearance, dietary habits etc., of new neighbors.

Identity strains and crises may occur when a child from a small village of rather simple social patterns moves into a busy, complex, multiethnic, multiracial urban apartment dwelling. Special problems are posed for children who come from rather deliberately limited social groups, especially those religious groups which as part of their upbringing of children insist that the children know as little as possible about the outside world. Certain religious sects in Pennsylvania have, for generations, encouraged their children to know little of the outside world. Such children may have social shocks at times when moving into another area.

Special hardships come to a family where a move is necessitated by economic difficulties. A rapid series of blows may be experienced by the family if the father has first lost his job, then had a vicious cycle of financial reverses as money stopped coming in and emotionally important belongings had to be sold or thrift had to be sharply and newly imposed. Perhaps ultimately the home had to be sold and life taken up under distinctly more modest circumstances. The life of a child formerly accustomed to a servant, to the leisure and tranquility that his mother may have delighted in because of the servant, may now find himself required to assist in a multitude of unaccustomed household chores in alliance with his possibly disgruntled and certainly newly fatigued mother. Such combinations of difficulties are necessarily more than additively burdensome. They tend to be experienced as an avalanche rather than as a stream.

When parents know that father is about to lose a job or has already lost one, no time should be wasted in explaining to the children (in age-appropriate ways) that they will be expected to help and in turn the parents will do everything possible to make it as easy as they can for the children. Hope is always to be kept in the forefront during discussions with children, *provided* there is at least some realistic basis for hoping that circumstances will once more improve.

The move which results from economic hardships is always accompanied by emotional distress among adults. The best protection for children under such circumstances is to share and understand adult emotional processes. If they are kept out of adult feelings and adults' lives they will see what is going on anyway and will notice mother's and father's worried expressions. They will overhear discussions about bills which are unpaid. They will, of course, notice that father does not go to work and probably will overhear plenty of bickering about these dilemmas. A child's adaptation (even a toddler's) is much easier if some of these matters are explained and he is allowed to ask as many questions as his mind can conceive. Any child who is speaking sentences can be told: "Daddy is getting a new job," or "We are going to get a new house," or "We will have different places to sleep." If his own bed arrangement will be changed, he should know about it at least a few days ahead of time.

A human being cannot abandon a loved person without a deep psychological wound. There is always mourning, even for a person who is both loved and hated. So it is also for our environment and physical surroundings. Whether or not we have been completely happy in our surroundings, nevertheless we have invested considerable amounts of psychological energy in thoughts and feelings about our surroundings. This energy must be gradually reinvested in order to permit us to make zestful and successful use of new environments. Many adults catch themselves feeling inexplicably sad after a move, although they consciously feel the move is for the better. Children are less likely to feel that a move is for the better and will resent the burden of making new psychological investments. Parents can be helped by becoming aware that even young preschool children become disgruntled following a move. Parental tolerance may be the only medicine necessary for this phase of discontented remembering to pass.

For a child who is less than three years old, the environment may have functions of what Winnicott calls a "transitional object." Very young children literally love such objects as teddy bears or blankets while they are learning to dissolve the primitive unions of very early life between child and mother. A physical environment probably receives some of the same loving given to teddy bears and blankets. A child cannot hug or go to sleep touching all of his house or sucking on an edge of the room, yet it can be comforting to him to see it and be in it. When he is away he may feel frustrated love and sadness for the now-distant house.

Although a child may not show that he is in any way disturbed by the move, the move is almost certainly noticed by any child more than a few weeks of age. Some children have so much experience in moving that it is part of their normal life pattern. Such children are not necessarily handicapped by frequent moves, and learn to put all their important psychological investments into their families rather than into their surroundings. Toddlers and younger children are likely to be so much more invested in their mothers and fathers and other family members than in their environment, that they will usually be less discontented about a move than older children, and especially less likely to have a period of prolonged discontent. However, if the adults are having difficulty in making moves, then a toddler's reaction may be quite severe. He is reacting to the adults rather than to the change of environment. The best remedy here, of course, is not an easy one; the adults must adjust to the environment.

The younger the child when moving, the more likely he is to take a step backward developmentally. Measures to prevent regression following a move should be especially directed to the mother-child relationship. The most serious regressions will occur when a mother has little time or attention to devote to a preschool child. Even some preadolescents and early adolescents may be quite vulnerable to mother's shifting her attention away from them for weeks (or months) at a time as she starts to furnish and decorate a new home. It would be wise to make sure that mother has a special time with preschool children every day. Father may have to disappoint his wife upon returning home from work in the evening. Instead of immediately helping her with the increased tasks for the new home, he may find life is easier for everyone if he spends a half-hour with the children after dinner.

Reactions of adolescents to the loss of friends may be very strong. This may be an index of how far a child has been able to move out of his family circle. After all, the main life task of an adolescent is to separate himself from infantile ties with his family. In order to do so, he must make heavy psychological investments, in his peers. The sadness he feels upon losing his buddies or girlfriends is in direct proportion to the degree of shift he has made away from love for his mother and father in an infantile sense. Thus, adolescents, in a kind of mourning for their old friends, may experience a disguised depression which appears as a thoroughly uncooperative attitude. Reluctance or inability to help in the new home is not pathologic, provided it is brief. A sympathetic expression from parents that they understand what a great loss is, may help shorten periods of balkiness.

Assistance from the parents in accelerating new social relationships, particularly by application for membership in youth groups in the new environment may be helpful. No matter how worldly-wise the teenager was in his former environment, he may need a parent to make sure he does even such a simple thing as look through the telephone book to find the number of the local YMCA. Occasionally, because of adolescent shyness, an adult in the family may be better equipped to do the "searching" than the teenager and find out where there are families with appropriately-aged youngsters. Because of the regression which may occur even for an adolescent, unhappy weeks might otherwise go by in loneliness.

For an adolescent, particularly if the move takes place in the middle of the school year, there may be a decline in school performance. This can often be smoothed over by a parental conference with the school guidance counselor. Similar measures may be quite useful for grade-school families, and for those with younger school children. Some assistance in learning the local homework and study patterns may be needed in the early months following a move, a matter often overlooked until there is an overt school problem.

In psychologically marginal families, or in those with several very young children, it may be worth the extra financial investment to hire a mover who will do all moving without supervision. With such an arrangement, a mother need not even be present in the house all of the time (or even most of the time) when the move takes place. More desirable is the mastery of a changed environment through the full cooperation of all family members. Such participation tends to be more feasible with healthy families, who grow stronger with the experience. As so often occurs in other life strains, the emotionally sick may grow weaker from an environmental move while the healthy may gain from the exertion. This rule is not at all a general one. Some emotionally ill children will benefit transiently from breaking patterns of pathologic transactions with their peers.

When an Older Family Member Moves

Advantages and burdens are part of lifetime collaborations between generations. Forms of change in family composition are myriad. When a grandmother moves away, it may be in order to take care of a new infant in another section of the family. This gives rise to a special sense of loss among the children whom she has recently helped raise. She may have been, in fact, more of a mother to some of the children than their own mother. Childhood grief will then ensue, with all its potentialities for character building and character damage.

Generally when a grandparent or an older sibling leaves it is a time of growth rather than deterioration. Parents can facilitate this identity shift in a positive direction by verbalizing the change and formalizing some of the shifts in responsibility. It should be stated openly that certain tasks performed by the older person will now be performed by a younger one. There should be expressions of the sadness of the occasion if it is felt by the adults, but also an effort to participate vicariously in the new adventures of the older siblings—as they go off to college, work, or marriage. Efforts should be made to have younger children keep in good touch with departing members by correspondence if necessary, and visiting if possible. There is a sense of broadening horizons for young children as older ones go off. This should be a good part of life. Yet sometimes an older brother or sister has been a parent-substitute and then some trouble may ensue, particularly for toddlers and young school children. Such families can be advised according to the recommendations made in the discussions of parental illness (p. 13) and separation (p. 1). Some reasons for a grandparent's departure are dealt with in Chapter II, Illness in the Family. Grandparents, of course, are the relatives most likely to suffer from gradual mental deterioration which accompanies senility. Some changes are especially painful and intimately involve the children.

The decision to have a grandparent move in is often the result of a family catastrophe, such as the death of one grandparent. If possible, some delay in the move is always advisable, but life circumstances are seldom kind enough to permit this time for adjustment. Some fast talking may be necessary with the children. As indicated before, the franker the better. This is another of those many times when sharing the truth is healthy.

Another area in which trouble may brew (besides the shifts in privacy and authority) is in the finances. A clear and early working out of financial arrangements may save much difficulty. It should be decided what portions of table money, mortgage money, and maintenance money, are to be the new-arrival's share. In middle- and lower-income families even such details as electricity money and lawn-mowing money are none too trivial. The new arrival may quickly realize that his presence could be helpful in these respects. If he is to be strictly a financial burden because of his inability to contribute, then a clear statement of this fact (provided he is mentally competent to understand it) will be useful in clearing the air and preventing false expectations of assistance from him. (Sometimes a grandfather who is thought by family legend to have a mint stored up in his mattress has nothing but lint in it.) The domestic work contributions of the grandparent could be discussed very early too. Along with other discussions with adults, children should have financial arrangements explained to them, perhaps not long after the reasons for the move are discussed. It is easy to overlook the interest of children in practical and financial matters. Any child old enough to count to ten has an interest in money.

In helping the grandparent, aunt or uncle adjust to their new life in the family, some family habits should be spelled out clearly. Children's bedtime can be stated so that the newcomer understands that his radio ought to be turned down at that time if his room adjoins the child's. A night-prowling oldtimer may have to learn that the family children are easy awakeners and should tactfully be asked to confine his nocturnal wanderings to the most distant parts of the dwelling. Parents can expect themselves to be resentful of any uncomplimentary remarks made by grandparents, no matter how true. Some tolerance by the newly arrived adult for the temperaments of the children might be promoted if their personalities are described in some detail. Grandparents often become quite rusty in assessing stages of childhood development.

The arrival or departure of a grandparent is a kind of signal from life that life is identical with change. Some parents can be encouraged to speak to their children about the cycle of life and the fact that children are not the only ones who change. The changes are for the most part pleasant, advantageous, to be looked forward to. But it must be faced frankly that at least some of the changes the grandparent has experienced contradict the grandparent's wishes —especially if this is evident. In some cases it may be possible to point out the pleasure it is to be a grandparent, the easier time a retired man or woman has, the greater leisure, the freedom from parental responsibility with the simultaneous joy in participating with the grandchildren in their childish pleasures. Parents have an opportunity to teach children that they can face life in the form in which it confronts them. Children can be given a sense of the changingness of life. This is an immunizing process.

CHAPTER VI

Overstimulating and Horrifying Experiences

Review of the Literature

Overstimulating Experiences: Primal scene

THE PATIENT described by Freud in "From the History of an Infantile Neurosis (1918) observed parental coitus at age one and one-half, but that event only gradually took on a pathogenic significance by age four. By then, a phobia had been partly determined by these earlier impressions. In the interim another fateful event had occurred—sexual excitement with a servant who threatened the little boy with castration. The child's wishful fantasy of passive submission to his father in place of his mother was abandoned when the child concluded that the price of such a fulfillment would be castration.

Abraham (1913) and Hall (1946) also dealt with the pathogenicity of primal-scene observations. Abraham, reporting on a nine-year-old girl's night terrors subsequent to a primal scene, notes that the child's recent heterosexual masturbatory experiences had sensitized her to the incident. Hall notes that the night terrors of a seven-year-old boy not only depended upon his having regularly observed parental intercourse, but that the terrors occurred in a matrix of sadistic fantasies about coitus. The neurosis was not precipitated until the boy himself engaged in forbidden sexual pleasures. Furthermore, he was in the midst of intense oedipal problems at the time of the terrors' onset.

Interference with Sense of Reality

Selma Fraiberg (1952) provides vivid information concerning the development of symptoms following verified observation. of grandparents having intercourse. Fraiberg's detailed material, like Freud's illustrates how a multifactorial predisposition existed when primal-scene observation occurred.

The clinically evident neurosis began at age 26 months, shortly after the child's visit to her grandparents in another city. She began to awake screaming inconsolably, after a brief sleep, and would then remain "rigid and watchful the rest of the night," complaining that "de noises" bothered her when no one else heard any sounds. During the day she was terrified even of slight noises. Soon she seemed "completely out of touch with reality," insisting that her family's house was "not our house." Genital masturbation was abandoned. She began compulsive thumb-sucking and rubbing just above the genital area. A strange ritual developed of handing her mother a certain wastebasket. She discarded her toys and refused to play.

Preceding the fateful visit to her grandparents were: (1) A pattern of frequent but cheerful nightwaking since earliest infancy. (2) Precocious verbal intelligence, with a recently acquired vocabulary of sexual and anatomical terms such as "the vulva" and "the genitals" and "preganacy." (3) A series of genital examinations by the pediatrician, presumably accompanied by pleasurable genital sensations. (4) Overt envy of the penis of her brother, born when the patient was 23 months. Narcissistic injury was evident in the form of disappointment in her own penis-less state. (She made explicit complaints regarding her deficient condition at age 24 months) (5) Discovery by the patient of mother's bloody sanitary napkins in a wastebasket (cf. the strange wastebasket ritual noted above), with subsequent explanation by the mother that the patient, too, would use such napkins when she grew up. (6) Mutual masturbation with a little boy, discovered by the mother who thought the children were fighting. In alarm, the mother urged the boy to stop hurting her girl.

Other important predisposers to pathogenic influence were the patient's already existing fantasies. These were, of course, a major part of the perceptual and cognitive framework with which the little girl viewed and misunderstood the grandparents' intercourse. Analysis revealed that the child was filled with oral-sadistic urges toward her brother. During analysis she actually tried to bite her brother's penis. She had a fantasy that she had once been a boy who had been castrated at birth. Later these fantasies changed to the idea that females are castrated during penetration by the male —then, that females damage the penis during penetration. She considered the used sanitary napkin to be evidence of her mother having a piece of penis still left inside her vagina, a piece removed from her father.

When the patient viewed her grandparents' sexual act, her immature ego was not yet possessed with a strong sense of reality. It was not easy for her to be sure whether or not she was dreaming. Further, her observations appeared to be perceptual confirmation of castration being a real process. The grandfather appeared to be making a hole in the grandmother. It is also significant that the little girl, who was then away from home, lacked her parents' presence to support her frail reality-testing activities.

Witnessing Parental Suicide

Witnessing parental suicide efforts may include in its mixture of pathogenic factors the element of interference with sense of reality and therefore is appropriate for discussion here.

Rosen (1945) describes a patient whose sense of reality was damaged in connection with his mother's suicide attempt and surrounding circumstances. The patient was a twenty-seven-year-old man whose presenting problems included a feeling that the world around him and his own self were "fragmenting" and seemed unreal. His symptoms were of recent onset and associated with depression and suicidal fantasies. The acute episode had been precipitated by a broken engagement. Regular psychoanalysis was not undertaken because the patient seemed to be schizophrenic. After an interruption of treatment due to the patient's persistent nonpayment of bills, the patient developed a wry neck and the sensation that his head felt as if it were being "twisted from my body." Fantasies of venetian blind cords looking like "hangman's ropes" then appeared, together with remarks about how iodine was never kept in the medicine chest in his family, nor had there ever been keys with which to lock the bathroom door. The analyst deduced that the patient's mother must have made a suicidal attempt in the bathroom, probably by hanging. Suggestion of this possibility to the patient brought forth a "remarkable and violent flood of affect . . . convulsive sobbing . . . lasting for about ten minutes." A marked relief from derealization occurred, with increased accessibility to treatment as well.

The patient's father confirmed that the mother had made suicidal attempts several times during the patient's preschool years. The father reported that on one occasion when the patient was three, he had gone to work and an older brother had gone to school. The patient's nurse heard sounds in the bathroom and just managed to prevent the mother from strangling herself. It is unclear what the patient viewed at this time. The nurse was later discharged because her presence was a reminder of the episode, according to both parents. Furthermore, the father and nurse tried to convince the patient that he had only *imagined* the event or had experienced a "bad dream." The father believed it would be harmful to the patient to remember this episode and also wanted to keep it secret.

Rosen notes that Freud's concept of "traumatic fixation" has not been abandoned. This particular case illustrates such fixation as well as an unusual outcome of the ego's adaptive efforts. Repression failed, Rosen believes, and the patient simply felt that he had been given permission to speak of a memory of which he had known "in some way all along" and had not been truly restored. The patient had lived under constant "threat of being overwhelmed by his affect" associated with the experience. Since important figures in the child's life had insisted the event was unreal, a special variant of defense was forced upon the ego, a reversion to an older process—primitive identification with the hanging mother. Rosen believes that when affects stimulated by an experience cannot be dealt with through repression, they are then invested in the child's body image and "thus little of the original object cathexis of the experience is retained." As a consequence of this "traumatically fixed" process, sensations in the body occurred with each mental repetition of the event, with concurrent partial decathexis of the outer world and consequent experience of derealization.

There are similarities between Rosen's case and that reported by Fraiberg (in "A Critical Neurosis in a Two-and-One-Half-Year-Old Girl"). Derealization was an outcome following a deeply disturbing observation. In both cases the child's sense of reality was quite tentatively developed and easily succumbed to the perplexing special features of adult responses which were part of the experience. Fraiberg's child witnessed a primal scene in the dark, in the absence of her own parents, and heard the sexual partners expressing doubts as to whether the child had seen anything—thus reinforcing her own doubts as to the actuality of her observation. The child was also horrified by what she thought was a confirmation of her sado-masochistic fantasies regarding intercourse.

In Rosen's case the significant parental figures actually preferred the patient to use denial and foisted on the child a pattern of confusing reality with dream. Rosen believes that, in the transition from the preoedipal to the early oedipal phase, it is likely that there is a transition in the character of the ego's utilization of identification. This process is parallel to the development of reality-testing. Both reality-testing and the identification process are quite vulnerable to regression during this transition stage.

Mary Bergen (1958) describes a different vicissitude of reality-testing in the treatment of a four-year-old girl whose mother had been murdered by her father. The child was in an adjoining room at the time of the murder and heard her mother screaming. She then saw her mother running away from her father, partly covered with blood, telling the little girl to get away. The father attempted suicide immediately, but did not succeed.

Prior to this deeply complicated disaster, the little girl had already been described as having "the pinched face of an old woman," was "quarrelsome, impulsive," plotting and scheming to be in charge of other children and grownups. She had expressed her dread over her father's murderous intentions just the day before, and had warned her mother that the father would kill her. Bergen believes that this realistic assessment of her father's behavior reduced "the element of surprise" and thus protected her from a significant factor in the development of a traumatic neurosis." Among the child's pre-existing problems were bed-wetting until age four and a rather dangerous, possibly counter-phobic behavior of jumping from high places. Previous stresses and strains to which she had been subjected included being "strapped in her pram" a great deal until age 18 months. She slept in her parent's bed until age four, a time which she was given her own bed and simultaneously ceased her enuresis.

Following the murder of her mother, Ellen began using a pre-existing channel of tension discharge to a greater extent. She began "to take refuge in mobility." There was no effort on her part to overtly deny the realistic facts. She organized other children in playing the "murder game." This game, which lasted only a few days, was one which she directed, thus keeping herself at a distance from a process which she controlled and which contained no falsifications. Also, in an active direction, Ellen frequently mentioned to strangers that her mother was murdered by her father, but, as in the play activity, kept some distance by avoiding discussion of the murder with anyone to whom she was emotionally close. In the hearing range of adults, she told other children that they should not be naughty and indicated that her own mischief had caused her parents to fight. After a few months Ellen began washing her hands in a ritual involving a wringing motion and staring at them and moaning "Me 'ands, look at me 'ands." She had considerable separation anxiety and began dangerously darting into traffic.

Analysis began nine months after the murder and continued for eighteen months. It disclosed that a particular aspect of the murder took on special significance. The mother's order to the little girl that she get away became a symbol of "all the exclusions from intimacy with the parents, from the loss of the mother who turned to the new baby, to being shut out of the parents' sexual relations and their actual experiences of violence and death." The child's oedipal conflict was at its height when the mother's death occurred, and therefore her guilt about that death was extreme. Ellen was "not old enough when treatment began to have a truly internalized conflict" and "analysis therefore prevented a serious neurosis from developing." It seems that the handwashing ritual was suggestive of internalized conflict, but in any case the analysis was most timely and had a preventive function of real importance.

Bergen notes that Ellen "relived" her traumatic experience intensely, and this was possible for the child because her reality sense was so good that she did not feel threatened with regression of this function when "reliving." The analyst was able to help Ellen face feelings of helpless loneliness for her mother and father (the latter being hospitalized). As in Meiss's case of a fatherless boy (see Chapter III), a special feature of the analysis was the child's readiness to form an analyzable transference, probably because of the absence of parents in her real life. Ellen also was apparently able to relinquish fantasies that her mother was really still protecting and watching her from heaven, a wishful bit of denial of death's actuality, which often proves damaging when the split persists.

As in other cases reviewed here, Ellen developed fusion of prior problems with the pathogenic episode. For example, this child had noticed signs of menstruation in the past, and these memories were mingled with those of her mother's deadly injuries. It was possible for the analyst to explain to the child how two burdens were present in her mind although most children "had only one." Ellen was also relieved by dealing with her prebereavement wishes to get rid of her mother and have her father for herself, understanding how the murder had seemed to make her wishes come true. This element of burdensome wish-fulfillment is a regular part of pathogenic experiences.

The loss of a major love-object for any reason may be capable of undermining all future emotional development even when the psychological damage is not immediately evident. Observing the violent ending of a loved person's life adds a crushing load of overstimulating perceptions, plus conflict over the child's own homicidal impulses which have been excited by the real life example. When the murder of one love-object has been committed by another, the calamitous example of the latter's weakness in respect to homicidal impulses further undermines the child's ability to control similar impulses of his own. These, at least, are expectations which seem reasonable.

CASE HISTORIES

Brutality, Terror and Abandonment

Five-year-old Kenneth came to The Center for Preventive Psychiatry upon the referral of The Society for the Prevention of Cruelty to Children. He had been found in his small house trailer taking care of an infant baby brother and his comatose mother. His mother's skull had been fractured in a terrible fight, allegedly with her common-law husband, whose involvement in the beating was suggested by Kenneth's account and by his conspicuous absence from the community. When found by a neighboring housewife who had, by coincidence, come to visit the family, Kenneth had evidently been in charge of the mother and baby for about 48 hours. The infant's skin was covered with numerous circular burns, seemingly from cigarettes. Emergency measures for these children's psychological well-being were two-fold. First, Kenneth and his infant brother were provided with a reliable foster family, one which was fortunately so well selected that the possibility was present for their becoming permanent foster parents. This measure proved to be more valuable than the SPCC and The Center for Preventive Psychiatry could have first realized, since the story of Kenneth's prior separation experiences was not yet known. The second immediate measure was to institute preventively oriented play therapy sessions twice-weekly for Kenneth, in which he had an opportunity to play and talk with a child psychiatrist concerning his recent experiences of violence and horror.

As Kenneth's history was pieced together, the psychiatrist and social workers involved learned that Kenneth's mother had made several attempts at abortion in the past (allegedly self-induced) and that his baby brother had been unwanted. The mother had made efforts in the past to give up Kenneth's care, having tried to persuade the Department of welfare to take him. Failing to accomplish this aim, she had succeeded in getting her own mother and stepfather to take the child for several months, but that arrangement had been terminated by her mother's death from a liver ailment. Now pregnant with the child of a man other than Kenneth's father, the desperate woman entered into more obscure difficulties, which have not yet been unraveled but which eventuated in the beating. Not only was her skull fractured, her face beaten black and blue, but most of her front teeth had been knocked out in the ferocities, the proportions of which were indicated by blood spattered on every wall of each room of the house trailer.

Kenneth was first seen by a psychiatrist* about 60 hours after being found in his home. Charged with the intense emotions which his experiences must have stimulated, frightened as well as horrified, lonely as well as perplexed, Kenneth eagerly reached out to the psychiatrist who offered him the kind of help "a talking doctor can give a child." As if prepared in a sophisticated fashion to participate in expressive play therapy, Kenneth brought to his first session a talking parrot with a small tape recorder which exclaimed, "I'll knock your block off!" The toy apparently had been selected by him to convey to his doctor the violent mental content which needed to be mastered. In that very first session Kenneth stated that his father had knocked his mother's teeth out "because she lied." In close contiguity to this account, he told the psychiatrist that his mother had tried to drown his baby brother.

Kenneth was able to reenact the events without prompting by the therapist. His dramatic reenactments using dolls and puppets began in the first session, notes of which are excerpted here.

"He first went for the puppet drawer, immediately taking out the mother puppet—and the mother puppet gave the boy puppet several vigorous smacks on the head. The boy puppet cried . . . the smacks were made with full arm movements— and intense affective response. We then switched around and I took the mother and he took the

* Daniel Feinberg, M.D.

Daddy out—the Daddy gave the mother a tremendous beating to which the mother responded by covering her head and whimpering and crying. Then he made us put them aside . . . (Later) he had the mother puppet in his hand and I had the boy on mine and the mother started to vigorously beat the boy and the boy cried. Then, when the boy puppet was off my hand, the mother started to beat me directly, with an attack that lasted a minute. . . . It was unclear to me at this point exacty who was who. . . . He insisted repeatedly that I get up, and that I was the boy and I had to stand up, all the way up, straight up. As he passed by me into the waiting room, he had the mother puppet on his hand . . . and said, "You see, there is a split there, in the head."

At first Kenneth was seen twice weekly. Every clue was utilized to show him that he was feeling not only upset and frightened about the beatings, but also was feeling lonely for his mother and father. This was made possibly by his several spontaneous references to the address of his parents and his frequent expressions of wishes to have his old toys and especially a bicycle given him recently by his father. By the sixth session, external reasons required reduction of frequency to once a week.

"His mood throughout a good part of the session for the first time was . . . sadness. There was no longer the hyperactivity . . . or high pitched voice and he was not nearly so controlling and bossy. At first he asked me to fix his wooden airplane which had broken a wing . . . his father had given it to him . . . he asked me—referring to my previous comment about having missed him—why I missed him.
The devil puppet squeezed a baby puppet very hard by the head and picked him up and threw him up to the ceiling. The devil, also called a "monster," had beat the woman puppet previously . . . Superman took care of the monster by throwing him up to the sky. Kenneth asked for a woman puppet but couldn't use it. Then he went for the skeleton puppet and asked if that was Frankenstein. He attacked me with it, having it go for my face and jaw, squeezing with one hand . . . I asked if Frankenstein was trying to knock my teeth out and Kenneth said, 'yes.' "

Kenneth did not return so floridly to dramatic reenactment of his recent experiences until the tenth session. In the meantime he had give up some pathologic means of dealing with his tensions means which included bed-wetting and unprovoked attacks on other children, sometimes trying to choke them. He began to settle into calm attendance in a public kindergarten, and got along well with his foster family. In the tenth session, "the boy became sick and was 'weak in the stomach' from not having anything to eat. Clark Kent beat up the mother quite severely."

After twenty sessions, which external reasons required to be the limit of preventive intervention, Kenneth had surmounted the hyperactivity and agressivity which his foster mother noted earlier. It appeared both to the therapist and the foster mother that the sessions, with their emphasis on catharsis, had reduced the child's hyperactivity in an almost mechanical fashion. It was as if steam had been let out of an over-heated boiler. But the subtler and possibly far more damaging effects of Kenneth's experiences lay not in his heightened aggressive tensions, but rather in his unrequited yearnings and undischargable love impulses for his absent parents. To a considerable extent these were interpreted, but Kenneth developed a tendency to misperceive. He would think his father had been in a crowded store in which he and his foster mother had just been shopping. He began to believe that his father was a delivery man who had come to deliver bread. These wishful illusions would require many months of intensive work to correct. However, our offer to carry out the task was not immediately accepted because of external obstacles.

Witnessing Infanticide and Pedicide

In the first year of its existence, The Center for Preventive Psychiatry had the sad and abortive opportunity to treat three little girls who had witnessed a murder in their own family. The Center's experience was doubly unfortuate. Not only had the girls been exposed to horrifying and probably damaging perceptions, but The Center was helpless in its efforts to extend assistance to these children because of special resistances aroused in the families involved in the particular crises. As in other fields of medicine, an unsatisfactory state of the art does not exclude physicians from the necessity of recording the difficulties and shortcomings. Therefore, in the hope that these experiences may help in the ultimate construction of better techniques, relevant excerpts from these cases will be presented.

Two Little Girls Witness the Murder of Their Baby Brother and a Suicide Attempt by Their Mother

A distraught father and concerned aunt sought advice at the suggestion of a pediatrician. One month earlier, the mother had stabbed her infant boy to death and then tried to commit suicide. Hearing screams, the children and father ran into the baby's bedroom where they were met with the scene of horror, the mother lying in a pool of blood on the floor. The two girls were then six years and four years old. Since the time of her brother's murder and mother's resultant rehospitalization, the four-year-old girl had expressed great longing for her mother, crying openly at times, accompanying her tears with questions such as, "When is my Mommy coming home?" She seemed to understand that her brother was dead, and would openly pray for him. ("God bless my brother.") Formerly a very obedient little girl, who had been "ruled with an iron hand" by her mother, this youngster was now in the care of a lenient grandmother and aunt who were unaccustomed to disciplining her. She had become gradually quite disobedient and, in addition, she was now clinging to her father, whom she generally used to ignore. Her wish for the mother's company was coupled with the knowledge that her mother was in the hospital and that her father visited her mother there. She wanted to go there, wanted to know what kind of hospital mother was in, and what color the room was.

The older child expressed puzzlement about her mother's condition, but in a displaced way. "How come Mommy's leg is hurt, when she cut her wrist?" She referred here to the mother limping slightly on the way to the ambulance. Like her younger sister, she now regularly shared her father's bed and experienced a good deal of separation difficulty when going to school in the morning. Neither she nor her sister were told that the brother had been killed, but rather that he had "gone to Heaven." The older child said laughingly that she had been sent away from her brother at the moment he went up to heaven. The father believed she understood that the boy was dead and cited evidence that she understood "President Kennedy went to Heaven" when he had been shot.

During the first and only personal contact with the children's father and aunt, the adults were supported in their self-described efforts to help the girls. "We have tried not to deny or change the subject when they talk about their mother although it's hard and we fill up with tears. We can't believe it." However, it was also clear that the children were being given a rather ambiguous explanation with some deception, and that the adults were in a state of profound distress which they were naturally conveying to the little girls. It was suggested that the little girl come to a therapeutic nursery school and the older girl receive psychotherapy once a week. The treatment would have included a program of guidance for the adults. However, after a few weeks contemplation, the father turned down both offers although there was no financial obstacle since free treatment was available. Reasons for the inability of this family to accept the recommendations and available treatment program may become more clear when the next case is examined.

A Four-Year-Old Girl Witnesses the Fatal Beating of Her Brother

A pale, pretty, freckle-faced girl whose four-year-old coy charm was marred by an inward turn of her eyes came to see me one afternoon accompanied by her mother. Just two weeks previously, she had apparently been at home during a protracted series of beatings in which her favorite uncle fatally injured her brother. She spent most of the first session with an object or a finger in her mouth, talking little and sighing much. Her sighing was spoken about to her by the therapist as "the kind of breathing people do when they feel very sad, like when they don't have a brother to build blocks with any more" (said while she was dejectedly putting blocks together). At this point the child became more communicative, talking hesitantly and indistinctly about her dog and her dollhouse. During this first interview, the child's mother kept up a fairly continuous stream of chatter and interruptions of the child's play activities. In the second session the mother disciplined herself to greater inactivity in response to the therapist's request. Soon the child was able to stay in the room alone with the therapist at which point she began a series of clearly enunciated statements and ceased the finger- and object-to-mouth activities which had punctuated most of her behavior in the early moments of the second session as well as throughout the first.

"I can bounce the ball to you, not just throw it." (It turned out that her brother had taught her this.) "I had a dream about man-monsters and I woke up my auntie to take care of me . . . there were little lady monsters in it, too . . . I don't remember it so good, but the man monsters were bad and the lady monsters were good. I was in a car. Somebody was driving me and all the lady monsters were walking on my head. The man monsters were scary and had big eyes."

Falling silent, the child responded then to a comment that this was a scary dream. She agreed that it was, except that the lady monsters were not scary. The therapist asked if she ever felt "like a man was sort of a monster?" No reply came.. The therapist then added, "A child might feel that way if they saw a man doing something bad." Apparently responding, she elaborated: "My brother and I used to play games where he tried to scare me, but it was really fun. We'd run around and hide and I couldn't always find him. I'd look and look and I couldn't find him." Then the child and I continued playing, which occupied most of the session. In the midst of rolling a ball to me, she stopped to draw a monster which she crumpled up after managing a crude, roughly rectangular shape, with a ball as a head and two eyes in the ball. As if in direct association to this monster, she told me of her uncle's work and how "he plays with me and everybody plays with me and we have lots of fun." I sympathized with her having an uncle that was a lot of fun to play with sometimes and commented that since he wasn't around now she must be lonely for him sometimes even though he did some things that were scary.

She then played with my toy telephone and told me her uncle had called her two days before and she had spoken with him. Her brother also used to call her on the telephone, "but he can't any more." She was very reluctant to leave, borrowing several toys from me, including a puzzle which had a large cut-out of a boy and girl.

Among her comments was one of special import: "If I told you something, Mommy would be angry." This detail, the implications of which remain unknown, may be just the sort that causes the patient to be withdrawn from treatment by a parent. In this case, there is reason to believe that the child's brother was murdered as the climax to a series of beatings. Feeling responsible for having failed to interrupt the prior beatings, a guilty aura might surround the mother's efforts to come to grips with the ultimate crisis of her boy's death and her brother's jailing and trial. To the extent that a mother feels herself involved and to the extent that this attitude is unbearable, the communicativeness of a child is a threat to the mother's psychological defenses against guilt. Beyond the question of legal responsibility, the mother's superego activity of self-condemnation, may be raised to extraordinary intensity in such a setting.

It is likely that similar superego factors were at work in the family murder case described previously (p. 122). In that case the father could well feel justified in sharing responsibility for prediction and prevention of the murder (since the psychiatrist in charge of his wife's treatment considered her safe to be at home with her infant), yet his own super-ego activity may have been nearly remorseless. The task, in retrospect, might have been better performed in both families by omitting any emphasis on the children themselves until a strong supportive and accepting relationship therapy had been established with the remaining parent. Under those circumstances, literally psychologically life-saving therapy might have been permitted for their surviving children.

CHAPTER VII

Children in a National Crisis

THIS CHAPTER deals with an event familiar to all, and quite different in many external ways from the psychological emergencies described in the previous chapters. Yet the previously noted principles of management are applicable.

The assassination of President Kennedy in 1963 created a psychological crisis for most of the nation, as much for children as for adults. The author conducted an extensive study of children's reactions to that event, which has been reported in part in *Children and the Death of a President* (Kliman, 1965).

As a guide to management of children during the emotional emergency of any national crisis, the experiences of war-time English parents are most valuable. Those parents found that even during the most severe blitz conditions, even the smallest children remained calm and well-organized behaviorally as long as they were with their own parents and as long as those parents were engaged in the pursuit of sensible protective activities. Amidst air-raids the parents were presumably frank in their communication of obvious concern that anger existed and protection must be sought. Children were literally brought into the process of family survival through direct action.

In the Kennedy assassination, as in the Cuban missile crisis, our nation's parents, teachers, and therapists had little direct participation in the actual event. Most of the experience was initiated and organized through the mass communications media. Yet there were numerous opportunities to bring children into the process of family and group reactions to the President's death and the surrounding events.

The following study examines in some detail the interactions between two generations during the first minutes and hours after the assassination became known. It provides some further basis for reflection concerning the application of principles previously outlined in this volume—the desirability of sharing emotional experiences between adults and children and the influence of adults and children on each other in crisis.

In January, 1964, a questionnaire was sent to all teachers in the elementary and high schools in a suburban community in a Northeastern state; it asked the teachers about their own reactions and the reactions of their students on the afternoon of the assassination of President Kennedy. This was part of a comprehensive investigation conducted by a team of researchers of the Department of Child Psychiatry of the Albert Einstein College of Medicine.* Reported here are the responses of the elementary-school classroom teachers only. †

Twenty-five out of the thirty questionnaires distributed in the elementary schools of the community were returned by the teachers. These teachers had a total of 600 pupils. Although the information obtained is not extensive, it gives a description, in their own words, of what these teachers recall their reactions to have been, what they did, and how they perceived the children's reactions. It tells something of how the teachers acted and of their feelings about their responsibilities during a crisis.

There is some variability in the responses of the teachers and in their descriptions of the afternoon of the assassination, but more striking is the similarity of their remarks even to the choice of words used to describe emotions and reactions. There emerges from the data an idealized image of the teacher as being calm and controlled, "for the reason that I was an adult in charge of a group of children."‡ In less than a third of the questionnaires returned do the teachers report that they expressed their emotions. They seem to be saying that one of their responsibilities is to avoid any emotional display which might frighten or distress the children. Three-quarters of the teachers described their outward behavior, after hearing of the assassination as "calm," "controlled," or "forced composure." The most frequently used adjective to describe the children's reaction was "quiet." That this was the ideal is implied by the fact that some of the teachers added "mature."

---

* Principal investigators were Dr. Martha Wolfenstein, Dr. Gilbert Kliman and Mrs. Ann Kliman, with the assistance of Dr. Joseph Cramer and several of his department's fellows in Child Psychiatry.

† My thanks to Mrs. William Alston for her collaboration in assembling, correlating and describing these data, as well as for her original contributions to the study.

‡ Direct quotes from the teachers' answers to the questionnaire appear within quotation marks.

One-third of the teachers (eight of the 25) reported that they first heard the news simultaneously with the children while watching television. When asked about their immediate reactions to the news of the shooting of the President, most of the teachers reported "shock" (8) or "disbelief" (10). Five more teachers said "shock *and* disbelief," and two said "horror." One teacher also reported feeling immediate concern for the Kennedy family and for the welfare of the country. When asked about the reactions of the children to the news, the teachers reported "utter silence" to "talking and giggling."

Teachers with outwardly calm reactions (14): An apparent relation existed between the children's reactions, as reported by the teachers, and the teachers' outward behavior (as reported by themselves). Three teachers of kindergarten and first grade reported that they reacted with "controlled calmness" or outwardly calm." One even reported her outward behavior as "none." In turn, these teachers perceived little or no reaction in their children. A connection between the teachers' outward behavior and the children's reactions seemed to exist also in the remaining elementary school classes. More than half of all the elementary class teachers reported their outward behavior as "calm," "quiet," "forced composure," or "controlled." These teachers reported the majority of the children's reactions as "quiet"; some said "normal." One teacher, who reported "no noticeable reaction" in the children, said her own behavior was "calm." Another teacher stated that her class was "very quiet and solemn," and she herself was "extremely controlled."

One teacher who "tried to maintain calm" reports her children's reaction in a most perplexing fashion: "They were angry and threatening but all in a very quiet manner. This unusual calm was maintained until dismissal." A teacher who described her own outward behavior as "serious, very calm, quiet" reported "some buzzing" in the class, but they "went on with the lesson." Still another teacher maintained a "calm atmosphere while showing concern *quietly,*" and the students showed "no marked behavior differences until after dismissal. Then when pre-teen-age children met, girls in particular, there was some weeping."

Teachers with no report of outward reactions: Six teachers reported "none" as their outward behavior or left the question concerning their outward behavior blank. Their children's reactions were not clearly described. One of these teachers reported that the children discredited the account of another child, "but were shocked to hear the principal's report." Another teacher, who said nothing of her own outward behavior, reported the students' reactions as "excited, had difficulty concentrating." Another response of children reported by a teacher who claimed "no outward behavior" after hearing the news was "uncertainty of how they should react, incomprehension." The teacher's final comment was: "It didn't seem to affect them too much."

A teacher with contradictory outward behavior: One first-grade teacher made the initial decision not to tell the children (she had heard about it from another teacher), but when some of the children heard it from other children in the lavatory she decided to turn on the television set. She told them briefly that the President had been shot and that their *parents* would tell them about it. She reported that she herself was upset and "in a daze" although "outwardly calm." In order to cope with the situation she gave the children some art activities. Some of the children chose to watch television rather than participate in the art work. This teacher reported having tears in her eyes, feeling "great sorrow," "fear and apprehension" and having difficulty continuing teaching. She was reluctant to share her thoughts straightforwardly, despite her obvious reactions to the event ("I told them very briefly what had happened and told them their parents would talk to them about it"). Yet she turned on the information-spewing television and left it on. Her conflict apparently included the need to limit her own feelings of distress, the need to suppress her own behavior, and the contradictory needs to learn about and share some of the experience.

Teachers with intense emotion: A group of eight teachers reported intense feelings such as "horror," "great shock," "crying," or "near tears." Four of them, however, also reported their outward behavior did not reveal their inner emotion. One was a teacher who left blank the first question about her outward behavior. Another said her outward behavior was "controlled calmness." Another said she thought she was outwardly calm "although as I talked with the children there were tears in my eyes." One of these teachers said she "became extremely controlled, although I could hardly stop myself from crying." The other four teachers in this group reported their outward behavior as "silence, near tears," "quiet," or "quiet tears."

Despite their emotion, they made great, and perhaps partly successful, efforts to conceal it. It is interesting to note, therefore, that four of these teachers reported children weeping in the classroom. There were only two other reports of children weeping in the 25 classes, and one of these was reported to have occurred after dismissal!

Stages in learning about the assassination: An effort was made in the questionnaire to distinguish between reactions to the initial news that the President had been shot, and to the final announcement that he was dead. Of those who reported hearing of the shooting before the death (15), all reported "shock" or "disbelief" except for one teacher who didn't give her reaction. Then, upon hearing that the President was dead, some still experienced "disbelief." One felt "disbelief and silence," another "disbelief and fear." Three teachers reported they felt "sadness" or "sorrow," and one felt "sorrow, but no real upset." Two teachers said their immediate emotional response was "tears" or "near tears." Another group (7) said that they felt "shock" or "speechlessness" at the final announcement. Two teachers reported "fear" and "fear and apprehension." One teacher felt a "profound sense of loss, icy-cold." Many of these are the same teachers who reported their outward behavior as "calm," "controlled," or "none" (20 of the 25).

Lack of school administrative action: No teachers reported receiving specific instructions from the school administration about telling the children about the assassination. One teacher noted that the principal visited the class, but left no orders. Another principal asked for a "moment of reverence." Another suggested that the teacher continue as usual but that she remind the children to go directly home after dismissal. Six teachers first heard the news via the public system from the principal's office.

Efforts to conceal the news: Six teachers made an independent decision not to tell the children about the President's assassination. These were teachers of grades ranging from the first to the fifth. Only one of the teachers claimed to have succeeded. She took her class outside for the rest of the afternoon. The remaining teachers reported that the children learned the news from other children met in the halls or in the lavatory. One teacher said she did not make a decision not to tell the children, but "I did limit the amount of time watching the TV program."

Pupils' behavior: The second page of the questionnaire included a list of 23 kinds of behavior the teacher might have observed in the pupils of the class after the announcement of the assassination. The teachers were asked to check any she had observed. It is notable that although only two teachers spontaneously mentioned a child weeping when asked to describe the children's *reactions,* in the check-list six teachers checked "weeping" and two of these also checked "sobbing." One teacher said only that the children were "shocked" at the report of the shooting, then she checked both "weeping" and "sobbing." She offered a partial explanation. "One child wept after hearing others in the hall." She also said that she had her class take a spelling test after hearing that the President had been shot and that they "reacted almost mechanically."

Teacher-pupil behavioral correlations: Teachers whose own emotional reactions we rated as "minimal" checked a mean of 1.5 pupil behavior items observed in class. Teachers whose reactions we rated "moderate" checked a mean of 3.1 pupil behavior items. Teachers with "moderately strong" reactions checked a mean of 4.4 pupil reaction items. Teachers with "strong" emotional reactions checked a mean of 6.1 pupil reaction items.

In some cases the teachers who felt strong emotional reactions to the news reported their outward behavior to be "calm" or "controlled." But regardless of their calm behavior they observed more reactions in the children than the teachers who did not report having felt such reactions themselves.

There is also an increase in the number of pupil-behavior items observed with increasing age of the children. The teachers of kindergarten, first, and second grades checked an average of 1 reaction (unusual quiet," "expression of disbelief," "restlessness more than usual," or "fearfulness without definite content"). Third and fourth-grade teachers checked an average of 1.75 reactions, and fifth and sixth grade teachers averaged 3.5 reactions. All six incidents of reported weeping occurred in the fifth and sixth grades. This raises the question of whether the older children reacted more obviously as a result of their own greater awareness of the gravity of the event, or because the teachers shared their own feelings more openly with the older children, or a combination of both. The kindergarten, first- and second-grade teachers all described the class and individual behavior as "normal," "usual," or "quiet." One teacher said the children watched the television reports instead of doing the assigned art work, but she does not tell what the children said or how they reacted to what they saw on television. The other teachers may have made the assumption that the younger children were not, or should not be, occupied with the tragedy.

The questionnaires, although hardly sufficient for any general conclusions, do give an indication of how our elementary school teachers see themselves in a crises. The similarity of many responses, even of vocabularly, suggests a stereotype of teacher behavior, ideal or actual. This can be described as employing considerable restraint and maintaining calm and control during a crisis. It would seem to be intended, if successful, to evoke a mature crisis response in the children. One sixth-grade teacher labeled the children's emotional reaction "rather mature." Another teacher of a mixed fourth and fifth grade reported: "My children showed a maturity far beyond their years and past behavior." Still another fifth-grade teacher said the children's reactions were "very mature on the whole."

The assassination of President Kennedy had an emotional impact greater than any other national event during most of these teacher's careers.* It would have been possible for the teacher to have stepped out of the teacher-pupil role structure and to have reacted as just another American whose President had been killed by an assassin. The fact is that most of the teachers reported doing all they could to conceal their emotion. One may question, in so doing were they acting in the best interests of the students? It is clear that many of them thought so. For some, by their account, it required an immense effort of will to appear calm and controlled. As one teacher expressed it: "I apologized for not being in complete control of myself" (however, this was a teacher who had described her behavior as "controlled calmness") "and thus not being in proper condition to explain what had happened. I told them that everything would be okay. That they should go home and their parents would explain everything to them."

It is true that a few teachers reacted spontaneously to the tragic news, but they are a small minority. To illustrate the spontaneity of one teacher and its effect on both the children in her class and on

* It is possible that some had been teaching at the time of the death of Franklin Delano Roosevelt, although none of them mentioned it.

her principal, the following is taken from an interview with a second-grade teacher in a different community, about a year and a half after the assassination of President Kennedy:

> It was the *worst* possible way to hear the awful news. . . . [The custodian] came back after a while, 2:30 wasn't it? He came back and said: "The President is dead!" Just like that! You could have heard a pin drop! You know how when you don't want the children to hear something, it's the very time they're all quiet and listening? Well, I, I just couldn't stop it, you know, I haven't had but a couple of shocks in my life, and nothing, I never had anything affect me like this! I just burst into tears! The children, the children were amazed. They'd never seen me like that. We all sat down together and we cried, and we—they all cried, too. We had a, a real human relationship! They wanted to know what had happened. I said, uh, I didn't know anything but the person who did this was sick! When we could stop crying a little I decided to take them all to [the principal's] office to see if we could find out some details. We kind of composed ourselves and started down the hall. [The principal] met us halfway down there and said, "Go back to your room!" [In telling this, the teacher's voice indicated that she felt rebuked.] Then [the principal] said "You can say good-by to your children now and send them home!" I did, and I explained to them that they would find out the facts when they got home, and they, but they should expect to see people sad and maybe crying, on the way home, and their parents would be, too.

Whether this teacher's behavior that afternoon had the approval of the principal and the parents of the children in her class is uncertain. She did not conform to the ideal expressed by the teachers responding to the questionnaire. But it is reasonably certain that the children in her class knew a tragic event had occurred which made a strong emotional reaction appropriate, and were able at least briefly to express it in the company of their teacher and peers.

Summary and Conclusions

The reports of elementary school teachers regarding their own and their pupils' emotional reactions to the assassination indicate the following:

1. Teachers of the youngest children were generally the least overtly reactive, and teachers of the oldest children were most overtly reactive.

2. The mean ranges of pupil-reaction items reported by elementary school teachers indicate the smallest range of reactivity among the youngest children and the greatest among the oldest children.
3. Regardless of the children's age, when teachers had minimal reactions, their pupils tended to have a minimal range of reactions. Conversely, those children whose teachers had marked emotional reactions tended to have a wide range of emotional reactions.

It is not possible to separate the factors of pupil age and teacher reactivity. There is strong internal evidence to indicate that teachers felt a greater responsibility for self-control, with the younger pupils, and felt freer for self-expression with older pupils. Variations between teachers working with pupils at the same age level suggest that if a teacher is emotionally expressive or inexpressive, her children will tend to be so as well.

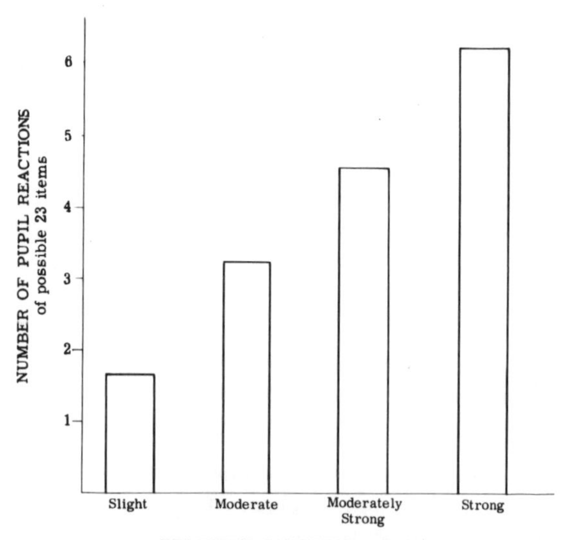

CHART 1

Implications for management of children during psychological emergencies depend upon the viewpoint and goals of such management. From a preventive psychiatric point of view, it seems desirable that in such a crisis there should be

1. Official communication of news by the teacher;
2. Controlled and limited but frank communication by the teacher of her own emotional reaction—at least of sadness, and of her own state of being in reaction to the event in other ways—such as thinking of what governmental procedures the nation would now use;
3. Opportunity for the children to express their own emotional responses in a controlled way within the framework of classroom activities;
4. Teacher and peer reassurance of particularly anxious or disorganized children.

What seems particularly undesirable is to avoid notifying children of a frightening event such as an assassination. School administrators who insisted upon this procedure, or teachers who themselves

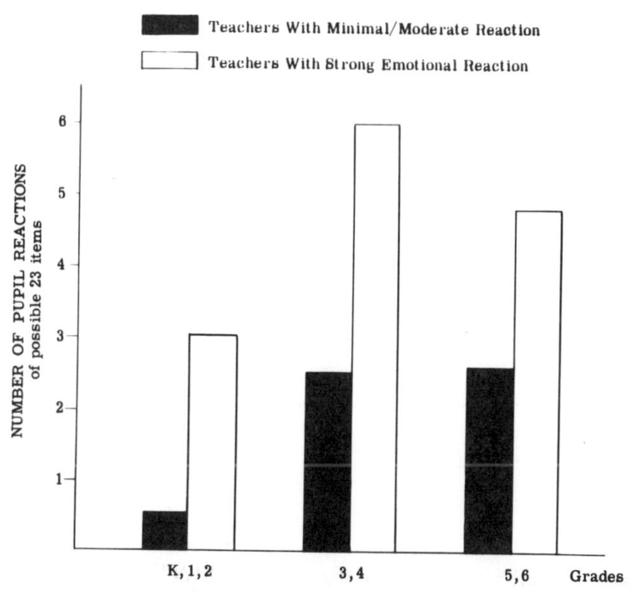

CORRELATION OF TEACHER AND PUPIL REACTIONS TO THE ASSASSINATION

CHART 2

elected to shield their pupils from the news did the children a disservice. Such children immediately heard the news from other children upon being dismissed or upon boarding the school bus (had they not earlier heard shoutings in the hall or learned garbled details from classmates who, in turn, had learned of the event during a trip to the bathroom). Instead of an organized situation in which to receive and react to the news, such children received a vote of "no confidence" from their teachers, who indicated they felt that the children somehow were not able to deal with the reality. Having received this demoralizing indication of deficient ability to deal with the reality, those same children were then required to deal with it—but under far less ideal circumstances than could occur within the classroom.

In this particular national psychological emergency and in the management of children within it are seen the same major principles which usually apply in cases of family tragedy. Generally, the sooner a child knows, the better he absorbs the news; the more participation in adult reaction, the better; the more opportunity to react with adult and peer support, the better; the more organized and supportive the adult-structured environment, the better.

CHAPTER VIII

Childhood Pathogenic Experiences

THERE ARE AREAS of curious inattention and inaction on the part of our culture and its therapeutic professions in regard to opportunities to prevent and minimize the effects of certain childhood emergencies. As a contribution to a more alert and systematic approach, this chapter will suggest an etiologic classification of childhood experiences in general, emergency experiences being included within the framework.

Psychogenic causes of psychiatric disorders are still debatable and poorly classified. The problem of classification is only slightly reduced if experiential factors are the sole focus. Even when further limiting the focus solely to intrafamilial experiences, the task is formidable. The latest report of the Group for the Advancement of Psychiatry states that "no classification can as yet be made of childhood psychological disorders in relation to specific pathogenic characteristics of the parent-child relationship."

Classification of pathogenic experiences is inherently difficult because of the myriad variables of contribution and response brought to an external event by the child who experiences it. These myriad variables are not only developmental and constitutional but also include countless prior experiential residues. However, it would be useful to *attempt* some approach to an etiological classification of parental and other experiential harms of childhood. For example, the following etiological classifications of potentially damaging experiences, although overlapping and certainly only partial, may provide a framework for rational preventive and minimizing interventions:

1. *Overstimulation experiences,* with subtypes according to duration (acute, chronic), type of stimulus, erogenous zone or modality involved, affect of the adult, and child's stage of development, i.e.: erotic clitoral overstimulation of an oedipal-stage girl by a loving adult male, chronic over a one-year period; or sadistic beatings of an anal-sadistic-stage boy on the anal region by an angry father. (For clinical examples, see cases in Chapter VI.) Precocious

puberty is an inner overstimulation experience which may lead to prematurely finding outer sources of sexual stimulation.

2. *Deprivation or deficiency experiences.*

a. Object deprivation, with subtypes according to duration, developmental stage of the child, sex of child, sex of parent, whether the deprivation is intermittent, permanent, due to separation or death, or to low emotional investment of the parent in the child.
(See Chapters I-IV.)

b. Specific stimulus or experience deprivation, i.e.: deficit of verbal communication when a child's mother is mute; deficit of visual stimuli and experience when a child is blind or has eyes bandaged; deficit of auditory experience when a child is deaf; deficit of kinesthetic and proprioceptive experiences, as in restriction of motility when a child is in traction or large casts.

c. Superego support deprivation, as when parents provide perplexing models of vacillation in impulse control (particularly in alcoholism and psychosis) or models of primary deficiency in superego function (as in psychopathic personalities). The effect is very different at different stages of superego development. Superego support deprivation may differ sharply in effect from interferences by the adult's seduction or contempt for the child's efforts to discipline his own impulses. A special kind of superego support deprivation is the experience of diminished esteem for the mental representatives of parents who have disillusioned a child. The ego ideal may be damaged, depending on its developmental completeness, autonomy, and the degree of disillusion.

3. *Experiences of parental interference* in the solution of normal developmental problems. The following list is only a small fraction of possible experiences:

a. Interference with appetite autonomies: under- or overfeeding, enforcement of limited or overly varied food choices, abrupt or overly prolonged weaning.

b. Interference with explorative activities: insufficient opportunity to move in the crib, see, touch, smell, or hear new stimuli; excessive encouragement to explore.

c. Restriction of toddling and walking opportunities.
d. Toileting interferences of many varieties, including the deprivation of opportunities for spontaneous experiments in fecal and urinary retention and timing of expulsion.
e. Interference with speech development by pressure to talk, excessively libidinized or hostile parental response to early speech, or deficit of spoken communication between parent and child.
f. Maternal interference with the task of mother-child separation.
g. Interference with superego development by harshness (see also Class 2 experiences, above) or by physical seduction or contempt for the child's efforts to control impulses.
h. Seductive parental interference with solution of the Oedipus complex.

4. *Fear experiences:* This category is restricted to situations in which a person is in real danger, as in a battle zone, when undergoing hazardous surgery, having a dangerous illness, or being imprisoned in a concentration camp where he may be killed at any time (see Chapter II).

5. *Prolonged anxiety or conflict experiences* which are beyond the ego's current ability to master, with subtypes according to the variety of anxiety or conflict (separation and castration anxiety are two common types), duration and developmental stage. These experiences often comprise responses to real situations which approximate a major fantasy of the patient. Conflict-involved libidinal or aggressive impulses contained within a fantasy may be expressed or reflected by the external world, with a consequent tendency to breakdown of a child's healthy defenses against those inner impulses. Often the external event is one which the child has helped to bring about, such as a seduction or series of beatings. Pathogenic effect may also occur retroactively when a prior experience becomes relevant to a new stage of a child's psychological development, conflicts and major fantasies.

6. *Endocrine abnormality experiences,* i.e., precocious puberty, delayed puberty. These experiences may be more purely "inner" rather than external life situations, but social transactions and opportunities for pathogenic experiences are markedly altered by such inner variations. Ultimately, as in other experiences, it is the inner solution which determines a healthy or disordered outcome.

7. *Interference with development of body image,* i.e.: Congenital deformity or stature abnormalities; surgical or accidental mutilation; cryptorchidism; neurological deficit or damage.

8. *Interference with cerebral function* as in toxic and other organic cerebral damage.

9. *Mixed and unlisted experiences:* Mixtures of the above experiences and unlisted experiential factors occur much more often than one experience alone. Example of a mixed type: a three-year-old child experiences the birth of a deformed sibling. He suffers guilty conflict over the expression in reality of a prior anal-sadistic fantasy regarding the unborn sibling, and suffers deprivation of parental affection during their period of depression following the deformed child's birth.

Any classification is inherently inadequate and difficult to use. What appears to be primarily one type of pathogenesis may, upon close inspection, be revealed to be primarily another. A previously virginal teen-age girl who was raped by her own alcoholic father several times in a two week period was not only overstimulated and conflicted. She also suffered covert deprivations. The covert deprivations consisted in the loss of her father as an acceptable parent, the loss of the value of memories concerning him, and the degradation of superego standards built up in prior years in association with him when he was less disturbed. These covert deprivations and the efforts to master them by distorted repetitions and reaction-formations against love for the degraded father wher probably more fateful than the obvious overstimulation and conflict aspects of her tragic experience.

Despite the inadequacies of the above-proposed classifications, certain preventive and mitigating measures can be rationally selected using such a framework. A schematic outline of measures available in working with psychologically endangered children includes the following:

A. *Examples of Primary Preventive Measures*

1. To prevent overstimulation, deprivation and developmental interference experiences: societal and parental *education* and supervision by "experts" in the field of child development and child treatment.

2. To minimize the pathogenic effects of fear, anxiety and conflict experiences which are anticipated: advance preparation of children by parents, doctors, teachers and others for expectable and situational crises. This preparation can be through verbal description and instruction, sharing of useful attitudes and information, synchronous with added support from age-appropriate object relations. (See Chapters I-V and VII.)

B. *Examples of Secondary Preventive Measures*

1. To master *current* experiences which are becoming or are already pathogenic: object substitution or experience substitution, supportive relationships, sharing of useful attitudes. Often possible for families as in A2. (See Chapters I-IV.)
2. Special technical measures for retroactive mastery of a variety of experiences which have already occurred.
3. Parent-guidance when parental interference with childhood development is detected.

Among primary preventive measures, the education of society at large, physicians, educators and parents, in particular, is currently the weakest and potentially the most practical and effective method. Essentially it may be defined as the application of psychiatric and psychoanalytic knowledge to child-raising techniques. Anna Freud has commented incisively upon certain limitations of such endeavors to date. She has clarified professional understanding of the high degree to which childhood fantasies, for example, of sexual processes, are apparently autonomous of adult efforts to bring those fantasies into closer approximation with reality.

The publication of works by Spitz (1951) Provence and Lipton (1962), and others regarding the adverse effects of deprivations such as prolonged mother-child separations and institutionalization in early infancy has helped to alter the grossly harmful practices of parents, orphanages and hospitals. To some extent, *primary prevention* of infantile psychopathology is thus actually occurring as a result of such advances. There is a real tendency of infant-caring institutions to recognize and honor the importance of providing maternal-like care for infants. This has even led to the procedure of assigning specific nurses to specific infants.

However, the influence of such seemingly convincing and compelling research as that of Spitz, Provence and Lipton has only moderately altered the illness-producing practices of medical and allied professions. The well-known primacy of early mother-child relationship constancy during early months is not uniformly honored by those who assume responsibilities for thousands of adoptions. The notorious Liuzzi case, in which a four-year-old girl was almost removed from her foster parents, illustrates the weak penetration of seemingly obvious principles. For example, adoption agencies in the metropolitan New York area have a tendency to delay adoption of infants for several months, using rationalizations that physical health checks are being made on the children, or the status of the prospective adopting parents is being investigated.

Even as this chapter was being prepared, the author took a history from a mother concerning her five-year-old psychotic girl. The baby had been kept in a metropolitan foundling hospital for eight months after birth while the mother (then unwed) debated about the child's fate. If the history given is valid, the infant was not allowed to be held by the mother while in the foundling hospital. She could only be viewed through glass, supposedly because of rules regarding physical hygiene. Yet there was not one nurse available with sufficient time to be a reliable mother-substitute.

Recently an adoption agency which was uncertain of its reasonably adequate psychological evaluation of a prospective parental couple consulted the author. During its period of indecision the adoption agency had kept the child in a foundling home for three months, with no constant person as a mother-substitute. The agency stated that this was a common period of delay in placement, and appeared distressed when the wisdom of such delays (even under circumstances of uncertainty regarding the prospective parents' emotional stability) was questioned.

Early life deprivations usually can be dealt with effectively only by prevention or swift reversal of the deprivation. Unfortunately, the earlier in life a severe deprivation occurs, the less susceptible it is to analytically-oriented treatment or corrective object relations. It is in this area where educational measures directed at society in general and parents in particular offer the greatest hope. Once a severe deprivation has occurred (for example, death of a mother during the child's infancy), from a psychiatric point of view there may be little that can be done directly with the child himself until he reaches age two or three. However, a good mother-substitute provided within a short period may prevent pathological sequelae of the object loss, and with continued good replacement even years later hope need not be lost.

Although parental loss may be looked upon as a deprivation experience, a certain view of it will reveal a kind of "overstimulation" experience in the sense that an unmanageable level of affect develops in the child. Urges formerly discharged upon the mental representative of the now-absent mother, for example, can no longer be discharged so readily upon a mental representative which reality-testing indicates is no longer present. Here, technical measures may be brought into play when the child is old enough to participate in therapy. These measures will be directed at releasing an affective tension which the child's unaided ego formerly could not discharge in bearable doses. This is a *secondary preventive measure,* aimed at preventing the long-range consequences of what Helene Deutsch (1937) has called "absence of grief." It is also important to strengthen the reality-testing function, lest it be overwhelmed by the wish to maintain a fantasy of a living parent.

Education has probably lessened the incidence of certain "overstimulations" which are thought (in our society) to have pathologic sequelae. A dramatic example is the tendency of many modern upper- and middle-class parents to carefully avoid exhibiting their sexual organs and activities to children. At another level of communication, removed from visible display of sexual activity, the same families are apt to provide their children with considerable intellectual sexual information. This is done with the expectation of strengthening the childhood capacity to cope with sexual urges and of preventing morbid sexual fantasies. There is as yet only reasonably based hope and little controlled evidence that experiential physical shielding combined with intellectual sexual education of children has the desired influence on their emotional health.

Experiences of overstimulation are also best dealt with by *primary prevention.* Such primary prevention could include social instruction and guidance of parents regarding avoidance of harsh punishments and primal scenes. Once an overstimulating experience has occurred, special technical measures may be used to lessen the likelihood of its becoming pathogenic. In addition to these technical measures, parents may be helpful to an overstimulated child if he has witnessed, for example, a primal scene. The child may believe he has had a nightmare. In the event of this misunderstanding, his parents could acknowledge that the event actually took place. In Chapter VI a case was reviewed in which a child's sense of reality was overwhelmed when the adults denied the primal scene had occurred (Fraiberg, 1952).

Conflict can be dealt with preventively by what might be called a process of psychological immunization through actual experience at a low-dose level. Intellectual mastery in advance is also useful in minimizing conflict experiences. Thus, for example, a child who feels himself deprived of maternal attention when a sibling is born commonly becomes conflicted about aggressive wishes he directs toward the sibling. If the child is already three or four years old, the experience may be one in which there is a powerful load of guilt, and this element of the experience may be more pathogenic by far than the deprivation aspect. Anticipating such an experience, the parents and family may prepare the child for his conflict at an intellectual level by speaking to him occasionally about the forthcoming birth. They can allow him to understand that mother will be busy with the new baby, and be sure not to completely conceal the hardship which will ensue. Whether through real experience, as with perceiving effects of sibling births in other families, or by discussion alone, the preparation can be done as in other immunizing processes in physical medicine. An antigenic stimulus is presented in a tolerable vehicle and at a dose sufficiently low so as not to cause a disease. The vehicle in this case is the affectionate interest of parents who advise the child in advance of some aspects of the situation he will soon face. When the experience or displacement by a sibling can be thought of anterospectively in verbal terms and can be shared with loving adults, the child learns a way to master it preventively. He may then respond more in a realm of shared verbal expressions, by telling the parents of his resentment rather than by raw action or private aggressive fantasy from which serious guilt is likely to ensue. Furthermore, the child who is prepared for such an event as sibling birth may be able to martial his defenses in a gradual and age-appropriate fashion, rather than needing to regress abruptly to disorganized and immature levels of adaptation.

The principle of mastery-in-advance applies equally well to adults facing an expected situational stress, but there is clearly a basic difference between the kinds of preventive measures which can be used for children and adults. In the case of children, the parents serve almost literally as auxiliaries to his various still-developing ego-functions. The borrowed strength of parental educative and supportive object-relationship is a crucial determinant in the child's reactions to what might be otherwise a pathogenic crisis. If, for example, parents in a disastrous storm or an air raid remain calm or engaged in constructive activities, the child is likely to accept this behavior as evidence that the situation is manageable. His level of anxiety will remain tolerable, despite the immaturity of his ego and the resemblance of the experience to his anal-sadistic fantasies. If in the same disaster parents are disorganized and anxiety-stricken to the point of panic themselves, the child then suffers a twofold disorganizing experience —a confirmation of his own dread of being overwhelmed by external forces, and a deprivation of effective parental care upon which some of his ego-functions are dependent.

In cases of developmental interference, there is an especially clear difference between psychiatric measures which can be used for adults and those suitable for children. It is often possible to conduct secondary preventive work directly in the presence of interference experiences. Mothers who infantilize or seduce their children during individuation or oedipal-phase development sometimes can be given emotional support by a child psychiatrist so that they can accept his guidance regarding the best mental hygiene for their children. It is possible to get mothers to allow their children to separate more, to share beds and bedrooms less, and even to do so without simply reshifting the parental pathology into an equivalent inroad upon the child's emotional development. Psychoanalysis of adults who happen to be parents may prove to be a powerful preventive measure in the psychological lives of their children. Probably the best preventive work concerning developmental interference goes on when there is a team—a child analyst for the child and an analyst for the parent most involved in the interference.

Bibliography

Abraham, K.: "Mental After-Effects Produced in a Nine-Year-Old Child by the Observation of Sexual Intercourse between the Parents." *In:* Selected Papers. London, Hogarth Press, 1913.

Barry, H., and Lindemann, E.: Critical ages for maternal bereavement in psychoneuroses. Psychosom. Med., 22:166-181, 1960.

Beck, A. T., et al.: Childhood bereavement and adult depression. Arch. Gen. Psychiat., 9:295-302 (pt. 3), 1963.

Bender, L. Childrens Reaction to Death of a Parent *In:* A Dynamic Psychopathology of Childhood, Springfield, Ill., Thomas, 1954, pp. 172-195.

Bergen, M. F. Effect of severe trauma on a four-year-old child, Psychoanal. Stud. Child, 13:407-429, 1958.

Bergmann, T.: Observations of children's reactions to motor restraint. Nerv. Child., 4, 1945.

——: Children in the Hospital. New York, International Universities Press, 1965.

Blom, G., and Waldfogel, S.: Emotional implications of tonsillectomy and adenoidectomy on children. Psychoanal. Stud. Child., 7:126-169, 1952.

Bonaparte, M.: Five Copy Books (1939). London, Imago, 1950.

Bowlby, J., and Robertson, J.: A two-year-old goes to the hospital. Psychoanal. Stud. Child., 6:82, 1951.

Brown, F.: Depression and childhood bereavement. J. Ment. Sci. 107, 1961.

Calef, V.: On psychological consequences of physical disease. J. Amer. Psychoanal. Ass., 3:155-162, 1959.

Deutsch. H.: Absence of grief. Psychoanal. Quart., 6:12-22, 1937.

Eisendorfer, A.: The clinical significance of the single parent relationship in women. Psychoanal. Quart., 12:223-239, 1943.

Eissler, K.: The Psychiatrist and the Dying Patient. New York, International Universities Press, 1955.

Fenichel, O.: Specific Forms of the Oedipal Complex (1931). *In:* Collected Papers I. New York, W. W. Norton, 1954.

Ferenczi, S.: The Nosology of Male Homosexuality (1941.) *In:* Sex in Psychoanalysis. New York, Basic Books, 1950.

Fleming, J.: Activation of mourning and growth by psychoanalysis. *Int. J.* Psychoanal., 44:419-431, 1963.

Fraiberg, S.: A critical neurosis in a two-and-a-half year old girl. Psychoanal. Stud. Child., 7:245-246, 1952.

Freud, A., and Burlingham, D. T.: War and Children. New York, International Universities Press, 1943.

______: Infants without Families. New York, International Universities Press, 1944.

______: The role of bodily illness in the mental life of children. Psychoanal. Stud. Child., 7:69-82, 1952.

______: Discussion of Dr. John Bowlby's paper. Psychoanal. Stud. Child., 16:53-62, 1960.

Freud, S.: Leonardo da Vinci and a Memory of His Childhood. Standard Edition, 11:59-137, 1910.

——: Mourning and Melancholia. Standard Edition, 14:243-259, 1917.

——: From The History of an Infantile Neurosis. Standard Edition, 17:3-122, 1918.

Friedman, S., and Chodoff, P. Behavioral observations on parents anticipating the death of a child. Pediatrics, 32:4(P. 1). 610-625, 1963.

Furman, R.: Death of a six-year-old's mother during his analysis. Psychoanal. Stud. Child., 19:377-397, 1964.

Glueck, S., and Glueck, E.: Unraveling Juvenile Delinquency. Cambridge, Mass., Harvard University Press, 1950.

Greer, S.: Study of parental loss in neurotics and sociopaths. Arch. Gen. Psychiat., 11.2, 177-180, 1964.

Gregory, I.: Anterospective data following childhood loss of a parent. Arch. Gen. Psychiat., 13:99-120, 1965.

——: Anterospective data following childhood loss of a parent. II. Pathology, performance and potential among college students. Arch. Gen. Psychiat., 13:110-120, 1965.

G. A. P.: Psychological Disorders in Childhood. Group for the Advancement of Psychiatry, Rept. No. 62, New York, 1966.

Hall, J.: Analysis of a case of night terror. Psychoanal. Stud. Child., 2: 189-227, 1946.

Hartmann, H.: Comments on the scientific aspect of psychoanalysis, Psychoanal. Stud. Child., 13:127-146, 1958.

Hilgard, J., and Newman, M.: Strength of adult ego following childhood bereavement. Amer. J. Orthopsychiat., 30:788-798, 1960.

Jessner, L., and Kaplan, S.: Emotional Reactions to Tonsillectomy and Adenoidectomy: Preliminary Survey. *In:* Problems of Infancy and Childhood. New York, Josiah Macy, Jr., Foundation, 1949, pp. 97-118.

——, and Blom, G.: Emotional implications of tonsillectomy and adenoidectomy on children. Psychoanal. Stud. Child., 7:126-169, 1952.

Kliman, G.: Bulletin No. 1. The Foundation for Research in Preventive Psychiatry, Port Chester, N.Y., 1966.

——: Oedipal themes in children's reactions to the assassination of President Kennedy. *In:* Children and the Death of a President (M. Wolfenstein and G. Kliman). New York, Doubleday & Co., 1965.

——: The Cornerstone Project, a Progress Report. The Foundation for Research in Preventive Psychiatry, Port Chester, N.Y., July 1967.

Kris, E.: Recovery of childhood memories in psychoanalysis. Psychoanal. Stud. Child., 11:54-88. 1956.

Kris, M.: Personal communication, 1964.

Levy, D.: Psychic trauma of operations in children. Amer. J. Dis. Child., 69:7-25, 1945.

Lussier, A.: "Analysis of a boy with a congenital deformity. Psychoanal. Stud. Child., 15:430-53, 1960.

Marris, P.: Widows and their Families. London, Routledge & Kegan, 1958.

Meiss, M. L.: The Oedipal problem of a fatherless boy. Psychoanal. Stud. Child., 7:216-229, 1952.

Morrisey, James R.: Death anxiety in children with a fatal illness. Amer. J. Psychiat., 18:600-615, 1964.

Nagy, M.: The child's theory concerning death. J. Genet. Psychol., 73:3-27, 1948.

Neubauer, P.: The one-parent child and his Oedipal development. Psychoanal. Stud. Child., 15:286-309, 1960.

Nunberg, H.: Principles of Psychoanalysis (1932). New York, International Universities Press, 1955.

Pearson, G. H. J.: Effect of operative procedures on the emotional life of the child. Amer. J. Dis. Child., 62:716, 1941.

Piaget, J.: Judgment and Reasoning in the Child. New York, Harcourt, Brace, 1928.

Planck, E.: Leg amputation in a four-year-old. Psychoanal. Stud. Child., 16:405-422, 1961.

_____: Death on a children's ward. Med. Times. 92:638-644, 1964.

Provence, S., and Lipton, R.: Infants in Institutions. New York, International Universities Press, 1962.

Remus-Araico, J.: Some Aspects of Early-Orphaned Adults' Analysis. (New York Psychoanalytic Society Lecture, September 15, 1964.) Psychoanal. Quart., 34:316-318, April, 1965.

Robertson, J.: A mother's observation on the tonsillectomy of her four-year-old daughter: with comments by Anna Freud. Psychoanal. Stud. Child., 11:410-436, 1956.

Roe, A.: The Making of A Scientist. New York, Dodd and Mead Co., 1953.

Rosen, V.: Reconstruction of a traumatic childhood event in a case of deprivation. J. Amer. Psychoanal. Ass., 3:211, 1955.

Shambaugh, B.: A study of loss reactions in a seven-year-old. Psychoanal. Stud. Child., 16:510-522, 1961.

Solnit, A. J., and Provence, S.: Modern Perspectives in Child Development. New York University Press, 1963.

Spitz, R.: Psychoanalytic diseases in infantry: An attempt at their etiologic classification. Psychoanal. Stud. Child., 6:255-275, 1951.

Vernick, Joel, and Karon, Myron: Who's afraid of death on a leukemia ward? Amer. J. Dis. Child., 109: 393-397, May, 1965.

Wilder, J.: Personal communication, 1959.

Index

Date D